Sally Kent. 50.

Ken L Gist

£1.50

€1·50

# MACBETH

Edited by Michael Davis

Marlborough College, Wiltshire

Illustrated by Colin Winslow

D0625171

LONDON   EDWARD ARNOLD (PUBLISHERS) LTD

© MICHAEL DAVIS 1964
*First published 1964*
*Reprinted 1968, 1971, 1972, 1973, 1975, 1979, 1980, 1982, 1982, 1983, 1984, 1986*

ISBN: 0 7131 1127 5

THIS EDITION IS FOR MY SON ROBERT

## THE KENNET SHAKESPEARE

Macbeth
Julius Caesar
Richard II
As You Like It
Romeo and Juliet
Henry IV, Part I
Twelfth Night
Henry V
The Tempest
The Merchant of Venice
A Midsummer Night's Dream

# ACKNOWLEDGEMENTS

I wish to acknowledge, with gratitude, my great debt to editions of *Macbeth* by G. L. Kittredge, Kenneth Muir, J. H. Walter and J. Dover Wilson; to M. C. Bradbrook's article, *The Sources of Macbeth*, in *Shakespeare Survey 4*; and to these books:

John Cranford Adams, *The Globe Playhouse*
A. C. Bradley, *Shakespearian Tragedy*
Cleanth Brooks, *The Well Wrought Urn*
W. C. Curry, *Shakespeare's Philosophical Patterns*
G. R. Elliott, *Dramatic Providence in Macbeth*
Helen Gardner, *The Business of Criticism*
A. Harbage, *Shakespeare's Audience*
C. Walter Hodges, *The Globe Restored*
Leslie Hotson, *Shakespeare's Wooden O*
G. L. Kittredge, *Witchcraft*
G. Wilson Knight, *The Shakespearian Tempest* and *The Wheel of Fire*
L. C. Knights, *Explorations* and *Some Shakespearian Themes*
Kenneth Muir, *Shakespeare's Sources*
M. M. Reese, *Shakespeare*
William Rosen, *Shakespeare and the Craft of Tragedy*
A. P. Rossiter, *Angel with Horns*
Paul Siegal, *Shakespeare and the Elizabethan Compromise*
J. I. M. Stewart, *Character and Motive in Shakespeare*
Roy Walker, *The Time is Free*

I am also very grateful to Bernard Harris for directing me to published works on *Macbeth*; to my wife and to Arthur H. White, Arthur E. Meikle and Iain Macdonald-Smith for their criticisms and suggestions; to John Nevinson for advice on illustrations; to G. Kempson for reading the proofs; and to members of the Hundred B form at Marlborough College in 1962 for their lively help. The drawing on page 53 is after a photograph by permission of the Governors of the Royal Shakespeare Theatre.

# INTRODUCTION

This is a play about the power of evil to corrupt, harden and destroy a sensitive human being. Its theme is as modern as that of any play which is being acted for the first time tonight, but Shakespeare (1564–1616) wrote for an audience of his contemporaries, and their ideas and interests influenced the way he presented his theme.

The play begins with three weird characters, the Witches. They would certainly have frightened Shakespeare's audiences, because witchcraft was generally believed in and greatly feared: only if you believe in the power of witches can you feel anything like the tremendous impact that this opening scene must have made on King James I, his Queen and his courtiers at the performance in Whitehall Palace in 1606. Mortal witches were people who, to gain supernatural powers, had sold themselves to the devil. These particular Witches are supernatural: they foretell the future, materialise and vanish as they please, conjure up apparitions and, most important of all, utter incomplete truths about the future which urge Macbeth towards murder and ruin. They speak in riddles, their truths sound like lies, and they have uncanny knowledge of Macbeth's evil desires. They are far more awe-inspiring than the mortal witches whom King James I had interrogated in Scotland before he ascended the English throne; he was fascinated by witchcraft and wrote a book about demonology.

The earliest text we have of *Macbeth* seems to have been prepared for a performance at court, and so our first drawing is set there. Judged by modern standards, scenery and effects were simple: actors relied upon the power of their lines to cast a spell; and Shakespeare's lines, spoken with conviction and relish, still cast their spell today. Some of his words have dropped out of our vocabularies or changed their meanings, and some of his phrases are obscure in their richness: but if you concentrate on the gist of the lines and read them aloud obeying the punctuation, many of the language difficulties dissolve in the dramatic music. The speeches should follow each other without delay, and you should not pause at the end of a line unless there is a punctuation mark. Speak expressively and swiftly, and the play will come to life.

[ 4 ]

# PRINCIPAL CHARACTERS IN ORDER OF SPEAKING

Three Witches
DUNCAN, King of Scotland
MALCOLM, his elder son
A Sergeant
LENNOX, a nobleman
ROSS, a nobleman
MACBETH, General of the Scottish Army
BANQUO, General of the Scottish Army
ANGUS, a nobleman
LADY MACBETH, Macbeth's wife
FLEANCE, Banquo's son
A Porter
MACDUFF, a nobleman
DONALBAIN, Duncan's younger son
An Old Man
Three Murderers
HECATE, Goddess of Witchcraft, usually omitted in performance
Three Apparitions
LADY MACDUFF, Macduff's wife
A Boy, their son
An English Doctor
A Scottish Doctor
Lady Macbeth's Lady-in-Waiting
CAITHNESS, a nobleman
SETON, an officer attending Macbeth
MENTEITH, a nobleman
Old SIWARD, Earl of Northumberland, General of the English
    Army
Young SIWARD, his son
                        and
Lords, Officers, Soldiers, Attendants, Servants and Messengers

# MACBETH

### *In open country, or above it on storm-clouds*

Shakespeare's plays, as originally printed, did not show the locality of scenes: *Macbeth* was first published in 1623, in the memorial volume of his collected plays and poems called the First Folio. Later editors have studied the plays and deduced where each scene is set. Shakespeare, who produced his own plays and sometimes acted small parts in them, wrote for a theatre that did not possess elaborate scenery: open country could have been indicated by a rock on a bare stage.

The witches are full of terrible power; their general aspect and some physical details are given in 1.3.39–47. These creatures seem, in 1.3.79, to be part of the wild, natural world: modern producers usually dress them in rags, but James I may have seen them in strange, symbolic costumes. Their rhyming speech, consisting of short lines with an irregular rhythm, creates an ominous effect.

3 *hurlyburly*   tumult of battle.

4 *lost and won*   finished decisively; but the witches speak in riddles which seem to confuse opposites. There are many quibbles or 'equivocations' of speech in *Macbeth*.

8 *Graymalkin*   a gray cat's name. The first witch's familiar, a cat, has just called her. A familiar is an intermediary between a witch and the spirit world.

9 *Paddock*   toad; the second witch's familiar.

10 *Anon*   immediately; the third witch will hurry away at her unspecified familiar's summons.

11 This is an epigrammatic summary of the witches' creed. To them, good is evil and evil is good, beauty is repulsive, ugliness is attractive. Moral confusion, reversal of desire and loathing, and contradiction of appearance by reality, are elaborated as the play develops. The emphatic rhythm of this line, with heavy and light syllables alternating regularly, drives home the importance of what the witches are chanting in chorus. Their rhythm, called trochaic, is made up of units (*feet*) consisting of a stressed syllable followed by an unstressed: Shakespeare gives this short scene compelling rhythmic power by his flexible use of it.

12 Do the words need stage effects of fog and mist? The witches go in different directions, and the hurlyburly of civil war rings out.

# MACBETH

## ACT ONE

## SCENE ONE

*Thunder and lightning. Enter three* Witches

FIRST WITCH: When shall we three meet again
  In thunder, lightning, or in rain?
SECOND WITCH: When the hurlyburly's done,
  When the battle's lost and won.
THIRD WITCH: That will be ere the set of sun.　　　　　5
FIRST WITCH: Where the place?
SECOND WITCH:　　　　　　　　Upon the heath.
THIRD WITCH: There to meet with Macbeth.
FIRST WITCH: I come, Graymalkin!
SECOND WITCH: Paddock calls.
THIRD WITCH: Anon.　　　　　　　　　　　　　　10
ALL: Fair is foul, and foul is fair:
  Hover through the fog and filthy air.　　　　[*Exeunt.*

antithesis.

## Macbeth

### A camp

S.D. (means 'stage direction' throughout) *Alarum* military trumpet call. *within* off-stage.

Like sequences in a film, Shakespeare's scenes generally follow on without a pause: in his day there may have been no interval during a performance. A banner can set the scene; Duncan speaks as soon as he enters and the blank-verse poetry begins. Its rhythm is iambic: each regular foot consists of an unstressed syllable followed by a stressed. Shakespeare varies this beat with supreme skill, throwing emphasis where meaning and emotion demand it.

1 *bloody*.  'Blood' is a key-word in this play, reinforcing in poetry the violence of the plot.

2 *his plight*.  Shown by limping and staggering, as well as by fresh gore.

3–6 The characters are unobtrusively sorted out.

7–24 Notice the construction of this news-report: 7–9, general situation; 9–15, build-up of Macdonwald's evil power; 16–20, relentless approach of valiant Macbeth; 21–3, brisk triumph of the hero. Why do we share Duncan's enthusiasm?

9 *choke their art*  obstruct their skill in the water.

10 *to that*  to that end; to make him one.

12 *Western Isles*  Hebrides.

13 *kerns . . . gallowglasses*  lightly-armed and heavily-armed Irish troops.

14 *Fortune,*  the goddess who is notoriously unreliable. *quarrel* cause.

15 *Showed*  appeared. *whore*  immoral woman, proverbially fickle. *Showed like a rebel's whore*  deceived him (aptly, because he was a rebel) by encouraging him with smiles, and then forsaking him. *all's too weak*  the rebel forces, helped by Fortune, are too weak for Valour's darling (*minion*), Macbeth.

16 *name*  title of 'brave'.

17 *Disdaining Fortune*  disregarding the goddess's help to the rebels; see l.14.

18 *which reeked with slaughter.*

19 *minion*  favourite.

20 The sergeant's broken lines, here and later, may indicate passionate excitement, pain or exhaustion.

21 *Which*  who (probably referring to Macbeth).

22 *ripped him open from the navel to the jaws.*  *unseamed* is a metaphor from clothes. The sergeant uses rugged and extravagant speech.

21–2 The ironically polite line and its brutal successor shock by their violently contrasted tones.

24 Duncan and Macbeth were grandsons of King Malcolm, whom

## SCENE TWO

*Alarum within. Enter* KING DUNCAN, MALCOLM, DONALBAIN,
LENNOX, *with* Attendants, *meeting a bleeding* Sergeant.

DUNCAN: What bloody man is that? He can report,
As seemeth by his plight, of the revolt
The newest state.

MALCOLM:                    This is the sergeant
Who, like a good and hardy soldier fought
'Gainst my captivity. Hail, brave friend!                    5
Say to the king the knowledge of the broil
As thou didst leave it.

SERGEANT:                    Doubtful it stood,
As two spent swimmers that do cling together
And choke their art. The merciless Macdonwald—
Worthy to be a rebel, for to that                    10
The multiplying villanies of nature
Do swarm upon him—from the Western Isles
Of kerns and gallowglasses is supplied;
And Fortune, on his damned quarrel smiling,
Showed like a rebel's whore: but all's too weak;                    15
For brave Macbeth—well he deserves that name—
Disdaining Fortune, with his brandished steel,
Which smoked with bloody execution,
Like Valour's minion carved out his passage
Till he faced the slave;                    20
Which ne'er shook hands, nor bade farewell to him,
Till he unseamed him from the nave to the chaps,
And fixed his head upon our battlements.

DUNCAN: O valiant cousin! worthy gentleman!

Duncan succeeded. Shakespeare found the history for this play in the *Chronicles of Scotland* by Raphael Holinshed (1587).

25 *reflection*  shining.

25–8 as shipwrecking storms break from the east, where the kindly sun rises, so strife bursts out from a place of apparent victory. You never can tell who will attack you next.

30 *skipping*  nimble; a scornful description of the Irish mercenaries mentioned in line 13 and its note.

31 *Norweyan lord*  King of Norway. *surveying vantage*  seeing his chance. Duncan's loyal troops were disorganized in victory.

34–5 *Yes . . . lion.*  Heavily ironical.

35 as sparrows frighten the king of birds, or a hare frightens the king of beasts.

36 *sooth*  truth.

37 *cracks*  charges of powder.

40 *Except*  unless.

41 or make famous another scene of death: a new 'place of the skull', where Jesus was crucified. There is much religious imagery (metaphor and simile) in this play, stressing and enriching the theme of sin and damnation.

46 *Thane*  a man who ranked with the sons of an earl and held lands of the king.

47–8 Lennox arouses expectation.

51 *Norway*  the King of Norway, Sweno. Shakespeare compresses, in time and place, the defeats of Macdonwald and Sweno. On the stage, details of history and geography are subordinated to drama.

SERGEANT: As whence the sun 'gins his reflection          25
 Shipwracking storms and direful thunders break,
 So from that spring whence comfort seemed to come
 Discomfort swells. Mark, King of Scotland, mark:
 No sooner justice had, with valour armed,
 Compelled these skipping kerns to trust their heels,          30
 But the Norweyan lord, surveying vantage,
 With furbished arms and new supplies of men
 Began a fresh assault.
DUNCAN:     Dismayed not this
 Our captains, Macbeth and Banquo?
SERGEANT:        Yes;
 As sparrows eagles, or the hare the lion. *not dismayed*          35
 If I say sooth, I must report they were
 As cannons overcharged with double cracks;
 So they
 Doubly redoubled strokes upon the foe:
 Except they meant to bathe in reeking wounds,          40
 Or memorize another Golgotha,
 I cannot tell—
 But I am faint, my gashes cry for help.
DUNCAN: So well thy words become thee as thy wounds;
 They smack of honour both. Go get him surgeons.          45
       [*Exit* Sergeant, *attended.*

*Enter* ROSS *and* ANGUS.

 Who comes here?
MALCOLM:   The worthy Thane of Ross.
LENNOX: What a haste looks through his eyes! So should he look
 That seems to speak things strange.
ROSS:      God save the King!
DUNCAN: Whence cam'st thou, worthy thane?
ROSS:      From Fife, great King,
 Where the Norweyan banners flout the sky          50
 And fan our people cold. Norway himself,
 With terrible numbers,

[ 13 ]

53-4 The Thane of Cawdor's aid to Sweno and Macdonwald
seems to have been entirely secret. Macbeth, in the next scene,
apparently does not know about Cawdor's deeds or plight.
54 *dismal* threatening.
55 *Bellona's bridegroom* Mars, the Roman God of War, husband
of Bellona. The classical name confers Roman valour on Macbeth. What more does Ross add to the impression of Macbeth
created by the sergeant? *lapped in proof* cased in tough armour.
56 matched Sweno as a warrior.
58 *curbing* restraining. *lavish* insolent.
60 *that* so that.
61 *composition* peace terms.

63 *Saint Colme's Inch* Inchcolm, an island in the Firth of Forth.
64 Dollars were sixteenth-century coins, but the historical characters shown in the play lived in the eleventh century: what ad-
vantages does a dramatist gain by using this sort of anachronism?
66 *bosom* dearest. *present* immediate.

## A heath

This scene was forecast by 1.1.1-6, and the crucial nature of
the witches' meeting with Macbeth was then implied. The
witches' plan for torturing an innocent sea-captain reveals their
spite and wide-ranging ability.

2 The death of farm-animals was commonly ascribed to witches.

6 *Aroint thee* scram! *rump-fed* fat-bottomed; or, fed on the best
joints. *ronyon* hag. The ronyon's mariner-husband will suffer
for this refusal of chestnuts.
8 *a sieve* the normal sea-going vessel of witches.
9-10 I'll turn myself into a rat—but incomplete (as transformed
witches tended to be)—and I'll slip aboard the *Tiger*, and cast
a spell on her.

Assisted by that most disloyal traitor
The Thane of Cawdor, began a dismal conflict,
Till that 'Bellona's bridegroom,' lapped in proof,                    55
Confronted him with self-comparisons,
Point against point, rebellious arm 'gainst arm,
Curbing his lavish spirit: and, to conclude,
The victory fell on us;—

DUNCAN:                     Great happiness!

ROSS: That now                                                       60
    Sweno, the Norways' king, craves composition;
    Nor would we deign him burial of his men
    Till he disbursed, at Saint Colme's Inch,
    Ten thousand dollars to our general use.

DUNCAN: No more that Thane of Cawdor shall deceive                    65
    Our bosom interest. Go pronounce his present death,
    And with his former title greet Macbeth.

ROSS: I'll see it done.

DUNCAN: What he hath lost, noble Macbeth hath won.

                                                    [*Exeunt.*

## SCENE THREE

*Thunder. Enter the three* Witches

FIRST WITCH: Where hast thou been, sister?

SECOND WITCH: Killing swine.

THIRD WITCH: Sister, where thou?

FIRST WITCH: A sailor's wife had chestnuts in her lap,
    And munched, and munched, and munched: 'Give me,'
        quoth I:                                                      5
    'Aroint thee, witch!' the rump-fed ronyon cries.
    Her husband's to Aleppo gone, master o' the *Tiger*:
    But in a sieve I'll thither sail,
    And, like a rat without a tail,
    I'll do, I'll do, and I'll do.                                   10

SECOND WITCH: I'll give thee a wind.

FIRST WITCH: Th'art kind.

14–17 I myself control all the other winds, and precisely the harbours they blow upon from every point of the compass-card.

18 *dry,* because the *Tiger* cannot put in for water: the witch will make the winds blow off-shore for 81 weeks.

20 *penthouse lid* eye-lid like a sloping roof.

19–20 The storm-tossed captain will get no sleep at all. Sleep is an important element in the play.

21 *forbid* cursed.

23 *peak* waste away.

24 Destiny will keep the *Tiger* afloat: this shows a limitation of the witches' power.

28 Bits of corpses were used in casting spells.

28–29 *pilot's thumb, Wracked* thumb of a pilot who was shipwrecked.

28–31 The four rhyming lines link the pilot ominously with Macbeth, a general who returns from guiding the ship of state through perilous seas.

30–1 The drum accompanies the troops: Macbeth and Banquo enter without them.

32 *weird sisters.* Except in line 6, no character speaks of witches. Euphemism makes them seem more elusive.

33 *Posters* speedy travellers.

32–7 This chant gives a running-commentary on the witches' actions. *Thrice to thine* three steps your way. Three and nine are mystic numbers. There were three Fates in classical myth: poets presented them as hideous old women.

37–8 Macbeth and Banquo, chatting as they enter, do not immediately notice the crouching witches, whose magic spell seems to have destined the meeting.

38 Macbeth, unconsciously adapting the witches' incantation of I.I.II, refers to the grim weather and grand victory, and perhaps also to the extreme change from defeat to triumph. The verbal echo suggests a mysterious link with the witches.

42–3 *aught That man may question* anything of which man may ask questions. Banquo fears that they are evil spirits.

44 *choppy* chapped.

43–5 The witches refuse to speak to Banquo yet. Perhaps they indicate that they want Macbeth to address them. During Banquo's speech has Macbeth shown emotions such as amazement, horror, fear, curiosity or disgust?

THIRD WITCH: And I another.

FIRST WITCH: I myself have all the other, 15
  And the very ports they blow,
  All the quarters that they know
  I' the shipman's card.
  I'll drain him dry as hay:
  Sleep shall neither night nor day
  Hang upon his penthouse lid; 20
  He shall live a man forbid;
  Weary sev'nights nine times nine
  Shall he dwindle, peak, and pine:
  Though his bark cannot be lost,
  Yet it shall be tempest-tost. 25
  Look what I have.

SECOND WITCH: Show me, show me.

FIRST WITCH: Here I have a pilot's thumb,
  Wracked as homeward he did come.      [*Drum within.*

THIRD WITCH: A drum! a drum!
  Macbeth doth come. 30

ALL: The weird sisters, hand in hand,
  Posters of the sea and land,
  Thus do go about, about:
  Thrice to thine, and thrice to mine, 35
  And thrice again, to make up nine.
  Peace! the charm's wound up.

*Enter* MACBETH *and* BANQUO.

MACBETH: So foul and fair a day I have not seen.

BANQUO: How far is't called to Forres? What are these,
  So withered, and so wild in their attire, 40
  That look not like th'inhabitants o' the earth,
  And yet are on't? Live you? or are you aught
  That man may question? You seem to understand me,
  By each at once her choppy finger laying
  Upon her skinny lips: you should be women, 45
  And yet your beards forbid me to interpret
  That you are so.

50 *hereafter*   in the future.
50–61 Macbeth starts fearfully and then stands lost in thought
while Banquo innocently consults the witches. Wonder may
suffice to keep Macbeth silent; or, if he has aspired to the crown
and even considered murdering Duncan to get it, feelings of
guilty horror grip him now. Macbeth's encounter with the
witches is the dramatic starting-point of his sinful career: but
the mysterious meeting does not explain *why* Macbeth responds
as he does. Man's proneness to sin is inexplicable. Shakespeare
shows us the startling growth of evil in Macbeth, not its funda-
mental origin.
52 Since 1.1.11, any 'fair' words spoken by the witches should be
suspect.
53 *fantastical*   imaginary.
55–6 *present grace . . . prediction Of noble having . . . royal hope*   the
thane-ship of Glamis, which Macbeth already has . . . the thane-
ship of Cawdor . . . the crown.
57 *rapt withal*   entranced by your greeting.
67 *get*   beget; be ancestor to a line of kings, although not necessarily be a king's father. King James I of England, who was King
James VI of Scotland, claimed descent from Banquo, a far more
attractive character in *Macbeth* than in Holinshed's Chronicle.
Shakespeare adapted history as he wished.
70 *imperfect*   leaving much unsaid. The witches gesture or move
to show that they are going: but 1.5.4 may imply that stage-fog
was used to cover their exit at the end of this speech, and perhaps
it began to rise now.
71 Sinel was Macbeth's father.
72–3 *the Thane . . . gentleman*.   Macbeth is either testing the
witches' knowledge or, more probably, he knows nothing about
Cawdor's secret, treacherous and risky aid to Sweno. See 1.2.53–4
and 1.3.108–16. The audience would be unlikely to wonder
about Macbeth's apparent ignorance: and Shakespeare wrote
for theatre-goers, not intentionally for students of literature.
76 *owe*   possess.
77 *blasted*   blighted.
70–8 *tell . . . Say . . . Speak, I charge you*.   Macbeth twice asks for
knowledge but finally commands it.

MACBETH:          Speak, if you can: what are you?

FIRST WITCH: All hail, Macbeth! hail to thee, Thane of
Glamis!

SECOND WITCH: All hail, Macbeth! hail to thee, Thane of
Cawdor!

THIRD WITCH: All hail, Macbeth! that shalt be King hereafter.                                                           50

BANQUO: Good sir, why do you start, and seem to fear
Things that do sound so fair? I'the name of truth,
Are ye fantastical, or that indeed
Which outwardly ye show? My noble partner
You greet with present grace and great prediction      55
Of noble having and of royal hope,
That he seems rapt withal: to me you speak not.
If you can look into the seeds of time,
And say which grain will grow and which will not,
Speak then to me, who neither beg nor fear             60
Your favours nor your hate.

FIRST WITCH: Hail!

SECOND WITCH: Hail!

THIRD WITCH: Hail!

FIRST WITCH: Lesser than Macbeth, and greater.          65

SECOND WITCH: Not so happy, yet much happier.

THIRD WITCH: Thou shalt get kings, though thou be none:
So, all hail, Macbeth and Banquo!

FIRST WITCH: Banquo and Macbeth, all hail!

MACBETH: Stay, you imperfect speakers, tell me more:    70
By Sinel's death I know I am Thane of Glamis;
But how of Cawdor? the Thane of Cawdor lives,
A prosperous gentleman; and to be King
Stands not within the prospect of belief,
No more than to be Cawdor. Say from whence             75
You owe this strange intelligence? or why
Upon this blasted heath you stop our way
With such prophetic greeting? Speak, I charge you.

[*The* Witches *vanish.*

**79–89** Banquo and Macbeth move about seeking the witches, and then come downstage (nearer the audience) to confer.

**81** *corporal* bodily.

**81-2** *melted As breath into the wind.* The simile adds a chill to the eeriness.

**84** *on* of. *insane root* root that sends its eater mad; hemlock, perhaps.

**86** It would be courteous of Macbeth to mention Banquo's destiny before his own: but perhaps he already shows anxiety about his own heirs.

**87** The mention of 'Thane of Cawdor' leads into the next episode, culminating at line 107.

**91** *the rebels' fight* quelling Macdonwald's rising.

**92-3** *his marvellings at your valour* struggle for expression with his desire to praise you. Silenced by that conflict . . .

**97** *images of death* corpses.

**98** *post* messenger.

**104** *earnest* pledge.

**106** *addition* title. Does Ross use the same gesture as the witches in hailing Macbeth?

**108-9** *why do you dress me In borrowed robes?* There are, in *Macbeth*, many metaphors and similes derived from clothes. Such imagery is apt in a play about the perplexing differences between illusion and reality: men are not what they seem, and hope is belied by achievement.

BANQUO: The earth hath bubbles, as the water has,
    And these are of them. Whither are they vanished?　　　80

MACBETH: Into the air, and what seemed corporal melted
    As breath into the wind. Would they had stayed!

BANQUO: Were such things here as we do speak about?
    Or have we eaten on the insane root
    That takes the reason prisoner?　*Banquo independant* 85

MACBETH: Your children shall be kings.

BANQUO: 　　　　　　　　　　You shall be King.

MACBETH: And Thane of Cawdor too; went it not so?

BANQUO: To the self-same tune and words. Who's here?

### Enter ROSS and ANGUS.

ROSS: The king hath happily received, Macbeth,
    The news of thy success; and when he reads　　　90
    Thy personal venture in the rebels' fight,
    His wonders and his praises do contend
    Which should be thine or his. Silenced with that,
    In viewing o'er the rest o'the self-same day,
    He finds thee in the stout Norweyan ranks,　　　95
    Nothing afeared of what thyself didst make,
    Strange images of death. As thick as hail
    Came post with post, and every one did bear
    Thy praises in his kingdom's great defence,
    And poured them down before him.

ANGUS: 　　　　　　　　　　We are sent　　　100
    To give thee from our royal master thanks;
    Only to herald thee into his sight,
    Not pay thee.

ROSS: And, for an earnest of a greater honour,
    He bade me, from him, ~~call thee Thane of Cawdor:~~　　105
    In which addition, ~~hail,~~ most worthy thane!
    For it is thine.

BANQUO: 　　　　What! can the devil speak true?

MACBETH: The Thane of Cawdor lives: why do you dress me
    In borrowed robes?

*from this moment Macbeth believes the witches*
*The same words* [21] *are used.*

112 *line*, another metaphor from clothing. *the rebel* Macdonwald.
113 *vantage* benefit.
114 *in his ... wrack* to ruin his country.

117 *behind* to come. Ross and Angus tactfully withdraw when Macbeth has thanked them.

120 *trusted home* believed absolutely. Banquo speaks lightly; he becomes serious when he says 'But 'tis strange . . .'
121 *enkindle you unto* make you hope for.
125–6 win us with correct information about trivialities, so that they can deceive us in matters of deep significance. Banquo, with clear-sighted honesty, perceives a truth which Macbeth does not discover until he is about to die (5.8.19–21).
127 *Cousins* friends; this greeting is frequently used by Shakespeare's nobles. Banquo joins Ross and Angus.
128 *swelling* increasing in splendour.
129 *imperial* royal. Macbeth sees himself as the hero in a play about a king. *I thank you, gentlemen* is a polite way of telling Banquo, Ross and Angus to move further off. They take the hint, and Macbeth can soliloquize freely.
130 *soliciting* prompting. Did the witches draw Macbeth on, or did he move of his own accord and excuse himself by blaming them?
131–3 But Banquo, following his wonder at 107, has just told Macbeth that 'The instruments of darkness tell us truths.' (124).
134 *suggestion* temptation. Has Macbeth been tempted to murder? Who suggested such a deed? Fate might somehow give him the throne without his intervention.
135 *horrid image*, of himself as Duncan's murderer. *unfix my hair* make my hair stand up. A mental 'image' terrifies Macbeth, although physical 'images of death' did not: see 1.3.96–7.
135–6 *hair ... make ... heart knock ... ribs.* These monosyllables have an impact which is almost physical.
137 in an unnatural way? Real causes of fear . . .

ANGUS:           Who was the thane lives yet;
But under heavy judgement bears that life     *110*
Which he deserves to lose. Whether he was combined
With those of Norway, or did line the rebel
With hidden help or vantage, or that with both
He laboured in his country's wrack, I know not;
But treasons capital, confessed and proved,     *115*
Have overthrown him.

MACBETH: [*Aside.*] <u>Glamis, and Thane of Cawdor:</u>
<u>The greatest is behind</u> [*To* ROSS *and* ANGUS.] Thanks for
your pains.    *The King is ahead / next*

[*Aside to* BANQUO.] Do you not hope your children shall be
    kings,
When those that gave the Thane of Cawdor to me
Promised no less to them?

BANQUO:           That, trusted home,     *120*
Might yet enkindle you unto the crown,
Besides the Thane of Cawdor. But 'tis strange:
And oftentimes, to win us to our harm,
The instruments of darkness tell us truths,
Win us with honest trifles, to betray's     *125*
In deepest consequence.
Cousins, a word, I pray you.

MACBETH: [*Aside.*]       Two truths are told,
As happy prologues to the swelling act   *display*
Of the imperial theme. [*Aloud.*] I thank you, gentlemen.
[*Aside.*] This supernatural soliciting     *130*
Cannot be ill, cannot be good. <u>If ill,</u>
<u>Why hath it given me earnest of success,</u>   *Fair*
<u>Commencing in a truth? I am Thane of Cawdor:</u>  *+*
<u>If good, why do I yield to that suggestion</u>  *foul.*
<u>Whose horrid image doth unfix my hair</u>     *135*
<u>And make my seated heart knock at my ribs,</u>
<u>Against the use of nature? Present fears</u>
<u>Are less than horrible imaginings.</u>

Although there was no spectacular scenery for Jacobean performances of Shakespeare's plays, costumes were lavish. The aim, however, was dramatic effect rather than historical accuracy—as in the plays themselves—and 'modern dress' was much used. In this picture of a performance at the Globe Theatre, Macbeth wears Jacobean armour and a plumed helmet which signifies his high rank. Banquo carries a similar but less grand helmet. Such costumes immediately tell Shakespeare's audience the status and nature of his characters. Ross's plaid is an adequate reminder that the men are Scots.

The Globe Theatre, an octagon of galleries round an open-air yard, with a wedge-shaped stage jutting out into the middle and a curtained inner stage behind that, was the permanent home of the King's Men. This theatrical company included some of the best players in England, and their own playwright, William Shakespeare, was the greatest in the world. He was also a co-director of the company, and he acted small parts. Duncan may have been one of them.

The leading actor was Richard Burbage, and Shakespeare wrote the great tragic roles for him. As Macbeth, in the drawing opposite, Burbage is near the front of the platform, which is 4 or 5 feet high and about 30 feet deep. Spectators would surround him on three sides, many of them—perhaps more than 500 out of a packed audience of about 2,000—standing in the yard: he is among them, and so his intimate speeches have personal impact. Behind him, the distant half of the platform is shielded by a gaily painted roof, supported on wooden pillars decorated to look like coloured marble. The Globe Theatre is designed to attract Londoners who want an exciting afternoon's entertainment.

139–41 *My thought . . . surmise* My thought, in which murder is still only visionary, so shakes the united kingdom of my manhood that the power to act is repressed by fantasy.

141–2 *nothing is . . . not* nothing is real except what I imagine.

130–42 Macbeth directly expresses his private thoughts and feelings. This dramatic convention, soliloquy, enables a character to meditate aloud while other characters on-stage cannot hear and are forgotten. It can greatly help a playwright, especially at turning-points in the development of character. In this soliloquy, we look beneath the great warrior's valiant appearance at his highly imaginative mind yielding to temptation and terrified by guilt. Is Macbeth sensitive, weak, scrupulous, unbalanced?

145 *our strange garments* one's new clothes. *their mould* the body.

147 the stormiest day ends sometime. Macbeth seems to dismiss his thoughts.

149 *favour* pardon. *wrought* agitated.

150 *things forgotten* things I was trying to remember; this lie is exposed to the audience by Macbeth's soliloquy.

151–2 *where every day . . . them* in my memory.

My thought, whose murder yet is but fantastical,
Shakes so my single state of man that function /action　　140
Is smothered in surmise, and nothing is
But what is not.
BANQUO:　　　　　Look how our partner's rapt. poetry
MACBETH: [*Aside.*] If chance will have me King, why, chance
　　may crown me,
Without my stir.
BANQUO:　　　　New honours come upon him,
Like our strange garments, cleave not to their mould　　145
But with the aid of use.
MACBETH: [*Aside.*]　　　Come what come may,
Time and the hour runs through the roughest day.
BANQUO: Worthy Macbeth, we stay upon your leisure.
MACBETH: Give me your favour: my dull brain was wrought
With things forgotten. Kind gentlemen, your pains　　150
Are registered where every day I turn
The leaf to read them. Let us toward the King. [*Aside to*
　　BANQUO.]
Think upon what hath chanced; and, at more time,

154 *weighed it*   given us time to weigh it.

155 *Our free hearts each to other*   our hearts freely to each other. Macbeth stresses *free*, but we know that his heart is already burdened. What is the difference between his reaction to the witches and Banquo's?

### In the palace at Forres

This is a state occasion: the King is going to announce his heir formally at a Council meeting, and so the scene opens with ceremony. A throne and a trumpet-flourish help to establish atmosphere, and a procession, symmetrical grouping, regalia and banners may increase it. Macbeth's arrival is unexpected: Duncan apparently intended to ask briefly about Cawdor's execution and then pass on to the royal succession.

2 *in commission*   given the warrant. Ross and Angus were sent to 'pronounce his present death' at 1.2.66.

9 *that had been studied in*   who had learnt by heart. *his death* how to die. The simile refers to an actor learning a death-scene. Shakespeare, a highly professional man of the theatre, often uses imagery from the stage.

10 so that he could throw away the most valuable thing he owned (his life).

11 *careless*   worthless.

5–11 This glowing tribute draws a disillusioned comment from Duncan: but the Sergeant's warning against false security (1.2.25–33), and the description of Cawdor's death, do not make Duncan wary of trusting. He is innocent, magnanimous and faithful.

12 by which we can discover the mind's true nature in the face.

13–21 *Macbeth* abounds in dramatic irony: when a playwright lets his audience know more than his characters do, he creates this type of tension. Here, Duncan confesses that he was deceived by Cawdor, but immediately greets Macbeth with generous, loving trust. We know Macbeth's treacherous thoughts, and so we feel the dramatic irony. There is much more of it later in this scene.

16 *Thou art . . . before*   your merit puts you such a long way ahead.

17 *wing*. Bird-imagery is important in *Macbeth*. Here it intensifies Duncan's pure gratitude.

[ 26 ]

The interim having weighed it, let us speak
Our free hearts each to other.

BANQUO: [*Aside to* MACBETH.] Very gladly.                    *155*

MACBETH: [*Aside to* BANQUO.] Till then, enough. [*Aloud.*
Come, friends.                                          [*Exeunt.*

## SCENE FOUR

*Flourish. Enter* DUNCAN, MALCOLM, DONALBAIN, LENNOX
*and* Attendants.

DUNCAN: Is execution done on Cawdor? are not
Those in commission yet returned?

MALCOLM:                         My liege,
They are not yet come back. But I have spoke
With one that saw him die; who did report
That very frankly he confessed his treasons,          *5*
Implored your Highness' pardon, and set forth
A deep repentance. Nothing in his life
Became him like the leaving it: he died
As one that had been studied in his death,
To throw away the dearest thing he owed             *10*
As 'twere a careless trifle.

DUNCAN:                       There's no art
To find the mind's construction in the face:
He was a gentleman on whom I built
An absolute trust.

*Enter* MACBETH, BANQUO, ROSS *and* ANGUS.

                   O worthiest cousin!
The sin of my ingratitude even now                    *15*
Was heavy on me. Thou art so far before
That swiftest wing of recompense is slow
To overtake thee. Would thou hadst less deserved,
That the proportion both of thanks and payment

19-20 *That the proportion . . . mine!* so that I might have been able to pay you in proportion to my gratitude.

23 *In doing it, pays itself* are their own reward.

24-5 *our duties . . . servants* our duties serve your throne and state with the natural affection of children and the loyalty of servants. Macbeth sums up the attitude of a loyal subject.

26 *Which* our duties, behaving like your children and servants.

27 *Safe toward your* which is sure to give you. Duncan and Macbeth exchange ceremonial speeches, but Macbeth's elaborate protestations sound hypocritical to us. Perhaps Duncan embraces Macbeth at 'Welcome hither'.

28 *plant* as in fertile ground, by making Macbeth Thane of Cawdor. But we have seen Macbeth contemplating advancement through unnatural violence, not through natural growth.

34 *Wanton* unrestrained.

35 *Sons, kinsmen, thanes . . .* Duncan masters his tears of joy and starts his royal proclamation, having shown by movement or gesture that he is about to speak of state affairs.

36 *nearest* nearest to the throne.

37 *We,* the royal plural. *our estate* the royal succession. Duncan has the right to choose his heir from among his close relations, who include Macbeth: in ancient Scotland, the king's eldest son did not automatically succeed. Now that the kingdom is secure, Duncan proclaims his heir and unwittingly provokes Macbeth.

39 *Prince of Cumberland* was the customary title of the heir to the Scottish throne. Cumberland was held in fee by Scotland.

41-2 *But signs . . . deservers* honours will be distributed widely.

42 Macbeth's castle is at Inverness. Duncan has turned to address his future host.

43 make me, as your guest, more indebted to you.

44 any leisure which I do not use for your service is hard work.

45 *harbinger* forerunner.

48-54 While Macbeth moves downstage and soliloquizes, Banquo praises him to Duncan.

48-9 *That is . . . down* Malcolm's promotion will trip me. Macbeth, thwarted by Duncan's proclamation, becomes more resolute in ambition.

50 *Stars.* Macbeth knows that murder is a deed of darkness: to attempt it, he must extinguish the 'signs of nobleness' in his own mind.

52 *wink at* be blind to. *be* be done.

52-3 *yet let . . . see* Macbeth is decisive. How and why has he changed since 1.3.134-142?

53 although the eye fears to see the murdered corpse.

50-4 The two rhyming couplets amplify the resolve expressed in Macbeth's soliloquy.

Might have been mine! Only I have left to say,　　　　20
More is thy due than more than all can pay.

MACBETH: The service and the loyalty I owe,
In doing it, pays itself. Your Highness' part
Is to receive our duties; and our duties
Are to your throne and state children and servants;　　25
Which do but what they should, by doing everything
Safe toward your love and honour.

DUNCAN:　　　　　　　　　Welcome hither:
I have begun to plant thee, and will labour
To make thee full of growing. Noble Banquo,
That hast no less deserved, nor must be known　　　　30
No less to have done so, let me infold thee
And hold thee to my heart.

BANQUO:　　　　　　　There if I grow,
The harvest is your own.

DUNCAN:　　　　　　　My plenteous joys,
Wanton in fulness, seek to hide themselves
In drops of sorrow. Sons, kinsmen, thanes,　　　　35
And you whose places are the nearest, know
We will establish our estate upon
Our eldest, Malcolm, whom we name hereafter
The Prince of Cumberland; which honour must
Not unaccompanied invest him only,　　　　40
But signs of nobleness, like stars, shall shine
On all deservers. From hence to Inverness,
And bind us further to you.

MACBETH: The rest is labour, which is not used for you:
I'll be myself the harbinger, and make joyful　　　　45
The hearing of my wife with your approach;
So, humbly take my leave.

DUNCAN:　　　　　　　My worthy Cawdor!

MACBETH: [*Aside*] The Prince of Cumberland! That is a step
On which I must fall down, or else o'er-leap,
For in my way it lies. Stars, hide your fires!　　　　50
Let not light see my black and deep desires:
The eye wink at the hand; yet let that be
Which the eye fears, when it is done, to see.　　　[*Exit.*

54 Duncan continues aloud his conversation which we have not heard.

55 and I feast on hearing him praised.

55–6 *fed . . . banquet.* The second word adds ceremony and lavishness to the first.

58 *peerless* unequalled.

Which qualities shown by Duncan in this scene do you regard as kingly?

### *Macbeth's castle at Inverness*

Perhaps Lady Macbeth appears reading the letter on the battlements, and descends later in the scene. See 1.5.37–9. The change from Duncan's blank verse to Lady Macbeth's prose gives variety and makes the letter seem realistic: she reads only the last part of it aloud.

1 *me.* We never hear Macbeth tell Lady Macbeth about the witches' prophecy to Banquo.

2 *perfectest report* most reliable information.

5 *rapt* See 1.3.57 and 142.

6 *missives* messengers.

10 *deliver thee* let you know.

11 *dues* due share.

12 Lady Macbeth clasps the letter, then secretes it somewhere on her.

15–29 Notice the construction of this speech: 14–15 declaration of confidence and fear; 16–24 analysis of Macbeth's nature in relation to evil; 24–9 impatient longing to fortify him for action. Does she, in 15–17, seem to despise a tender, gentle nature and dismiss it as weak, or does she only declare that it is unsuitable for a murderer? What did the letter show you about Macbeth's feelings for his wife? Her understanding of his character is revealed in 15–24: Holinshed called Macbeth 'somewhat cruel of nature', but Shakespeare presents a far more complex warrior.

16 *the milk of human kindness.* Milk is associated with motherhood, children, innocence, nourishment and helplessness. *Kindness,* here, implies good human feelings stronger than gentleness or benevolence.

17 *catch the nearest way* snatch by the most direct method.

17 *wouldst* would like to be.

19 *The illness should* the evil which should. *thou wouldst highly* you would like very much.

DUNCAN: True, worthy Banquo: he is full so valiant,
  And in his commendations I am fed;                    *55*
  It is a banquet to me. Let's after him,
  Whose care is gone before to bid us welcome:
  It is a peerless kinsman.              [*Flourish. Exeunt.*


# SCENE FIVE

*Enter* LADY MACBETH, *reading a letter.*

LADY MACBETH: 'They met me in the day of success; and I
  have learned by the perfectest report, they have more in
  them than mortal knowledge. When I burned in desire to
  question them further, they made themselves air, into
  which they vanished. Whiles I stood rapt in the wonder of   *5*
  it, came missives from the King, who all-hailed me, "Thane
  of Cawdor"; by which title, before, these weird sisters
  saluted me, and referred me to the coming on of time, with,
  "Hail, king that shalt be!" This have I thought good to
  deliver thee, my dearest partner of greatness, that thou   *10*
  mightest not lose the dues of rejoicing, by being ignorant
  of what greatness is promised thee. Lay it to thy heart,
  and farewell.'
  Glamis thou art, and Cawdor; and shalt be
  What thou art promised. Yet do I fear thy nature,          *15*
  It is too full o' th' milk of human kindness
  To catch the nearest way: thou wouldst be great,
  Art not without ambition, but without
  The illness should attend it; what thou wouldst highly,

20 *thou wouldst holily*   you would like to get by fair means.

21 *wrongly win*   win what you should not have.   *thou'dst have*   you would like to have.

22 the thing—the crown—which cries 'You must do this!' if you want it. Unlike her husband, Lady Macbeth pursues unhesitatingly the intention of murder.

23 *And that which*   and you would like that thing—the murder—to be committed which . . .

24 *Hie thee*   hurry.

26 *chastise*   whip.

27 *golden round*   crown.

28 *metaphysical*   supernatural.

30 Fate and the attendant seem to forestall her wishes: no wonder she is startled!

31 She tries to cover her guilty amazement with an excuse to the attendant.

32 *informed for preparation*   let me know so that I could prepare.

34 *had the speed of*   outrode.

35 *more*   more breath.

37 *the raven himself is hoarse.*   Even the hoarse raven, a bird of ill-omen, sounds hoarser than usual because it is forecasting Duncan's murder.

39 *my.*   Is there significance in Lady Macbeth's saying 'my' and not 'our'?   *Come, you spirits . . .*   In this appalling invocation to the powers of evil that the witches serve, Lady Macbeth probably clasps her hands in prayer or stretches out her arms in supplication.

40 *tend on mortal thoughts*   serve murderous thoughts.

42 *make thick my blood*,   and so prevent pity from flowing in my veins.

43 block the way that compassion might use to approach and enter me.

44 so that no contrite feelings of human nature.

45 *fell*   ruthless.

45-6 *keep peace . . . it*   restrain that purpose from its achievement.

47 and suck my milk and replace it with gall (a most bitter substance inducing harshness of spirit), you attendant spirits of murder.

48 *sightless substances*   invisible embodiments.

49 *wait on nature's mischief*   minister to the evil deeds of humanity.

46-9 If you believe that there are dark spiritual powers in the world, you are likely to sense the full horror of Lady Macbeth's prayer. She is performing a fervent, terrible ritual to pervert her womanly nature.

That thou wouldst holily; wouldst not play false,      20
And yet wouldst wrongly win; thou'dst have, great
    Glamis,
That which cries 'Thus thou must do', if thou have it,
And that which rather thou dost fear to do
Than wishest should be undone. Hie thee hither,
That I may pour my spirits in thine ear,      25
And chastise with the valour of my tongue
All that impedes thee from the golden round,
Which fate and metaphysical aid doth seem
To have thee crowned withal.

*Enter an* Attendant.

                     What is your tidings?
ATTENDANT: The King comes here tonight.
LADY MACBETH:               Thou'rt mad to say it.
Is not thy master with him? who, were't so,      31
Would have informed for preparation.
ATTENDANT: So please you, it is true: our Thane is coming;
One of my fellows had the speed of him,
Who, almost dead for breath, had scarcely more      35
Than would make up his message.
LADY MACBETH:             Give him tending:
He brings great news. [*Exit* Attendant.] The raven him-
    self is hoarse
That croaks the fatal entrance of Duncan
Under my battlements. Come, you spirits
That tend on mortal thoughts, unsex me here,      40
And fill me from the crown to the toe top full
Of direst cruelty! make thick my blood,
Stop up th'access and passage to remorse,
That no compunctious visitings of nature
Shake my fell purpose, nor keep peace between      45
The effect and it! Come to my woman's breasts,
And take my milk for gall, you murdering ministers,
Wherever in your sightless substances
You wait on nature's mischief! Come, thick night,

49–53 See 1.4.50–3.

50 *pall* shroud. *dunnest* darkest.

51 *my keen knife.* She envisages killing Duncan herself.

53 *Hold* stop.

53 If Lady Macbeth has been standing on an upper level so far during this scene, does Macbeth enter on the same level as her, or below?

54 *the all-hail hereafter.* What is the effect of this echo from 1.3.50?

56 *ignorant present* present which is ignorant of the future.

57 *the instant* this moment. Macbeth, like us, knows that she means murder.

57–60 Are there significant pauses in this dialogue?

57–8 He speaks with eagerness and awe.

59 *as he purposes.* Macbeth loads these words with reluctant implications that Duncan will die before the morrow.

59–60 *O never . . . see.* She destroys the ambiguity. Her prophecy will be fulfilled not only by Duncan's death, but also by an eclipse of the sun, 2.4.6–10.

61 *my Thane.* She speaks with affection, mastery and possessiveness.

62 *beguile the time* deceive the world.

63 *Look like the time* wear an expression that suits the moment.

64–5 *flower* and *serpent* emphasize the Eden-like temptation of a husband by his wife.

66–7 *provided for; great business.* Hostess and murderess unite in these euphemisms. Direct expression would be less horrible.

67 *dispatch* management. The verb 'to dispatch' means 'to kill', and so Lady Macbeth puns on the word. Shakespeare achieves many effects by double meanings. *Macbeth* abounds in this form of word-play, which appealed greatly in Shakespeare's very word-conscious age. Nowadays puns are thought suitable to comedy rather than to tragedy, but in *Macbeth* they are used for intensifying horror: the dramatist seems to be underlining a word with different coloured inks, and so enriching it emphatically, vividly and wittily. The wit has a serious, ironic effect.

69 *solely* absolutely.

70 Her appalling boldness made him lower his eyes.

71 a disturbed expression always arouses mistrust.

How has Lady Macbeth shown her power over Macbeth?

And pall thee in the dunnest smoke of hell,                    50
That my keen knife see not the wound it makes,
Nor heaven peep through the blanket of the dark,
To cry 'Hold, hold!'

               *Enter* MACBETH.

                      Great Glamis! worthy Cawdor!
Greater than both, by the all-hail hereafter!
Thy letters have transported me beyond            55
This ignorant present, and I feel now
The future in the instant.

MACBETH:                 My dearest love,
Duncan comes here tonight.

LADY MACBETH:          And when goes hence?

MACBETH: To-morrow, as he purposes.

LADY MACBETH:              O, never
Shall sun that morrow see!                  60
Your face, my Thane, is as a book where men
May read strange matters. To beguile the time,
Look like the time; bear welcome in your eye,
Your hand, your tongue: look like the innocent flower,
But be the serpent under't. He that's coming         65
Must be provided for; and you shall put
This night's great business into my dispatch;
Which shall to all our nights and days to come
Give solely sovereign sway and masterdom.

MACBETH: We will speak further.

LADY MACBETH:           Only look up clear:         70
To alter favour ever is to fear.
Leave all the rest to me.             [*Exeunt.*

*Lady Macbeth going to murder*

### Outside the castle entrance

Oboes provided delicate music in Shakespeare's theatre, and they were sometimes used to give an eerie effect. A gentle melody sharpens the irony of the unsuspecting victim's happiness in this scene.

Torches showed, at an open-air, daylight performance, that an episode occurred at night. This is not a dark scene, however, but a sunlit, evening one: torches are carried out of the murky castle to welcome the victim-king. They are needed, symbolically, in the black, hellish place that lies within the charming exterior.

1 *seat* situation.

3 *gentle senses* senses which are made calm (by the air).

4 *temple-haunting martlet* house-martin whose haunt is churches. *approve* prove.

5 *by his loved mansionry* by using it as his favourite building-site.

7 *coign of vantage* suitable corner.

8 *pendent bed* hanging nest. *procreant cradle* cradle for breeding.

1–10 These lines convey security and delight. The words *pleasant, gentle, guest, summer, temple, loved, heaven's breath, bed, cradle* and *delicate* are all associated with tranquillity and happiness. Not the raven but, ironically, the creative 'temple-haunting martlet' welcomes Duncan. Banquo's observant interest in birds and their ways adds pleasantness to his character. This lyrical interlude is made poignant by our fears for Duncan.

13 *yield* reward.

11–14 *The love that . . . for your trouble*—(Duncan explains with serene courtesy, in a speech full of dramatic irony, that this royal visit is a sign of his love for Macbeth and Lady Macbeth) —the love of our followers sometimes makes inconvenient demands on our royal person, but we are still grateful for that love. From this example I teach you to say 'God reward the King' for the work we now cause you, and to thank us for giving you the trouble of entertaining us.

15 *point* respect.

16 *single* feeble. *contend* compete.

19 *late* recent. *to* in addition to.

20 *rest* remain. *hermits* beadsmen, pensioners who pray for the souls of their benefactors. *Where's . . . Cawdor?* Presumably he could not face the ordeal of greeting Duncan.

21 *coursed* chased.

22 *purveyor* official who goes ahead to arrange a royal visit.

23 *love,* for Lady Macbeth. *holp* helped.

# SCENE SIX

*Oboes and torches. Enter* DUNCAN, MALCOLM, DONALBAIN, BANQUO, LENNOX, MACDUFF, ROSS, ANGUS *and* Attendants.

DUNCAN: This castle hath a pleasant seat; the air
  Nimbly and sweetly recommends itself
  Unto our gentle senses.
BANQUO:                    This guest of summer,
  The temple-haunting martlet, does approve
  By his loved mansionry that the heaven's breath        5
  Smells wooingly here: no jutty, frieze,
  Buttress, nor coign of vantage, but this bird
  Hath made his pendent bed and procreant cradle:
  Where they most breed and haunt, I have observed
  The air is delicate.

*Enter* LADY MACBETH.

DUNCAN:                    See, see, our honoured hostess!        10
  The love that follows us sometime is our trouble,
  Which still we thank as love. Herein I teach you
  How you shall bid God yield us for your pains,
  And thank us for your trouble.
LADY MACBETH.                    All our service
  In every point twice done, and then done double,        15
  Were poor and single business to contend
  Against those honours deep and broad, wherewith
  Your majesty loads our house: for those of old,
  And the late dignities heaped up to them,
  We rest your hermits.
DUNCAN:                    Where's the Thane of Cawdor?        20
  We coursed him at the heels, and had a purpose
  To be his purveyor: but he rides well,
  And his great love, sharp as his spur, hath holp him
  To his home before us. Fair and noble hostess,
  We are your guest tonight.

26 *in compt*   ready to be accounted for.

28 *Still*   always.

25–8 *Your servants ever . . . own*—(Lady Macbeth, with a gesture
of obeisance, declares that the king's subjects are stewards to
the king, always ready to account for the royal property en-
trusted to them. The subject owns nothing: the king owns
everything)—your servants always keep their servants, themselves and their possessions in readiness, so that when your
Highness wishes they can present an account and always give
back what belongs to you anyway. Lady Macbeth plays the part
of a loyal hostess: her facade of sweetness in this scene derives
either from callousness or self-control.

31 Duncan takes Lady Macbeth's hand.

How has this scene increased the dramatic tension?

### Inside the Castle

Perhaps musicians appear on the stage, following the torch-bearers.
The butler and servants move with ceremonial dignity suitable to
a royal feast. They go off to the banqueting-chamber from which,
after a pause, Macbeth enters. His first speech in this crucial scene
gives private and public reasons against murdering Duncan: 1–12,
murder is sure to be avenged; 12–16, I would be doubly disloyal
if I killed Duncan; 16–25, his virtues would arouse universal pity
for his death; 25–8, only ambition spurs me on.

1–2 *If it were . . . quickly*   if the murder were to be over and done
with as soon as it had been committed, then to do it quickly
would be a good thing.

3 *trammel*   enmesh, as in a net.

4 *his surcease*   Duncan's death.

5, 6 *here*   in this world.

7 *jump*   risk.   *life to come*   eternal life following death and judgement-day.   *these cases*   murders.

8 *still*   always.   *have judgement here*   receive sentence on earth.
*that*   in that.

9 *Bloody instructions*   lessons in bloodshed   *being*   after they have
been.

10 *inventor*   contriver who has taught others.   *even-handed*   im-
partial.

11 *Commends*   recommends.   *poisoned chalice*.   What are the implications of this agonizing image, with its deadly adjective and
sacred noun?

14 *Strong both*   both strong.

LADY MACBETH:                     Your servants ever                     25
  Have theirs, themselves, and what is theirs, in compt,
  To make their audit at your Highness' pleasure,
  Still to return your own.
DUNCAN:                     Give me your hand:
  Conduct me to mine host; we love him highly,
  And shall continue our graces towards him.                     30
  By your leave, hostess.                     [*Exeunt.*

*Duncan unsuspecting & trusting.*

## SCENE SEVEN

*Oboes and torches. Enter, and pass over the stage, a Butler,
and various Servants with equipment and food for a banquet.
Then, enter MACBETH.*

MURDER OF KING

MACBETH: If it were done, when 'tis done, then 'twere well
  It were done quickly: if the assassination
  Could trammel up the consequence, and catch,
  With his surcease, success; that but this blow
  Might be the be-all and the end-all; here—                     5
  But here upon this bank and shoal of time—
  We'd jump the life to come. But in these cases
  We still have judgement here, that we but teach
  Bloody instructions, which being taught return
  To plague the inventor. This even-handed justice                     10
  Commends the ingredients of our poisoned chalice
  To our own lips. He's here in double trust:
  First, as I am his kinsman and his subject—
  Strong both against the deed; then, as his host,

*If he could kill him & not get caught he would do it.*

17 *faculties* powers. *meek* humbly.
18 *clear* innocent.


20 *taking-off* murder.
22 *blast* storm of fury. *cherubin* cherubs, a higher order of angels. *horsed* mounted.
22–5 *heaven's cherubin . . . wind* the cherubs of heaven, riding on the invisible winds, shall reveal this murder to everybody, so that showers of piteous tears shall drown the storm of wrath.
25–7 *I have . . . ambition* I have nothing but bounding ambition to spur on the horse of my purpose.
27 *o'er leaps itself* vaults too violently into the saddle.
28 *other* other side.
1–28 Like Judas, Macbeth left his victim at supper; the soliloquy opens with an echo of Jesus' command: 'that thou doest, do quickly' (John 13: 27). Macbeth speaks with increasing intensity, and lines 19–25 present glimpses of judgement-day. Lady Macbeth evoked evil spirits (1.5.39–53) and Macbeth now visualizes angels and cherubs: the range of the drama extends to heaven and hell. The metaphors between 19 and 29 reveal, by their strength and compression, the overpowering visionary anguish of Macbeth's mind.


32–4 Macbeth speaks of honour and public esteem, not of hell—his most profound and disturbing argument against murder.
34 *would* should. *in their newest gloss* with the sheen of new clothes still on them.


36 *dressed* She challenges him in his own metaphor.
37 *it* the hope, like a drunkard with a hangover, afraid to fulfil the promises he made when he was drunk.
39 *Such* as worthless as a drunken promise. Perhaps she gestures scornfully.


41 *that* the crown.
43 *esteem* estimation.

Who should against his murderer shut the door,                    15
Not bear the knife myself. Besides, this Duncan
Hath borne his faculties so meek, hath been
So clear in his great office, that his virtues
Will plead like angels, trumpet-tongued, against
The deep damnation of his taking-off;                            20
And pity, like a naked new-born babe,
Striding the blast, or heaven's cherubin, horsed
Upon the sightless couriers of the air,
Shall blow the horrid deed in every eye,
That tears shall drown the wind. I have no spur                  25
To prick the sides of my intent, but only
Vaulting ambition, which o'er-leaps itself
And falls on the other—

*Enter* LADY MACBETH.

                                 How now! what news?
LADY MACBETH: He has almost supped: why have you left
    the chamber?
MACBETH: Hath he asked for me?
LADY MACBETH:                        Know you not he has?        30
MACBETH: We will proceed no further in this business:
He hath honoured me of late; and I have bought
Golden opinions from all sorts of people,     Macbeth was Honoured
Which would be worn now in their newest gloss,
Not cast aside so soon.
LADY MACBETH:                    Was the hope drunk              35
Wherein you dressed yourself? hath it slept since,
And wakes it now, to look so green and pale
At what it did so freely? From this time
Such I account thy love. Art thou afeared
To be the same in thine own act and valour                      40
As thou art in desire? Wouldst thou have that
Which thou esteem'st the ornament of life,
And live a coward in thine own esteem,

44 letting fear accompany desire.

45 *adage* proverb. The cat wanted fish but shrank from wetting its paws.

35-45 She 'chastises' him with taunts of cowardice and of not loving her.

45 *Prithee, peace* I pray thee, be silent. He is angry at being accused of cowardice.

46 *become* be becoming to.

47 *none* no man, but either superhuman or subhuman.

48 *break* disclose. When did he suggest the murder? Or is her question intended to deceive him? Macbeth, like the audience, would not have time now to consider who made the original suggestion.

50 *to be more ... were* to become king.

51 *more the man* more valiant, as she implies that an assassin would need to be.

52 *adhere* suit. *would* were determined to.

53 *that their fitness* their very suitability.

54 *unmake you* reduce you to a coward. *I have given suck.* Only a mother can truthfully say this. Macbeth and Lady Macbeth appear to be childless: they may, however, have had children who died in infancy. (Shakespeare does not present the historical fact that Macbeth was Lady Macbeth's second husband and that she had borne a son to her first.)

60 *But* only. *the sticking-place* the limit to which a soldier tautens the string of his cross-bow, or a musician the strings of his violin, or a murderer his courage before sticking in the dagger.

46-61 Macbeth produces a strong argument: excessive daring is indeed unmanly. Lady Macbeth realizes that this moment is critical, and makes a supreme effort at line 54. Spoken by a woman, such words are shocking; Macbeth is shocked, and shifts his ground at line 59. Immediately, Lady Macbeth knows that she has succeeded, and proceeds confidently with plans.

63 *chamberlains* attendants of the royal bedchamber.

64 *wassail* carousal. *convince* overpower.

65 *warder* guard. Memory was thought to protect reason, sited higher in the brain, against fumes rising from the stomach.

66-7 *Shall be ... only.* The guard itself will melt to an alcoholic vapour (*fume*) and the brain, receptacle (*receipt*) of reason, will become a retort (*limbeck*) for distilling alcohol.

68 *drenched* drowned.

70 *put upon* ascribed to.

71 *spongy* drink-sodden.

72 *our great quell.* She speaks as if this murder were a glorious enterprise. Compare Macbeth's words for it at line 20.

73 *mettle* spirit; also, material.

Letting 'I dare not' wait upon 'I would',
Like the poor cat i'the adage?

MACBETH:                              Prithee, peace:                    *45*
I dare do all that may become a man;
Who dares do more, is none.

LADY MACBETH:                        What beast was't then
That made you break this enterprise to me?
When you durst do it, then you were a man;
And, to be more than what you were, you would          *50*
Be so much more the man. Nor time nor place
Did then adhere, and yet you would make both:
They have made themselves, and that their fitness now
Does unmake you. I have given suck, and know
How tender 'tis to love the babe that milks me—        *55*
I would, while it was smiling in my face,
Have plucked my nipple from his boneless gums,
And dashed the brains out, had I so sworn as you
Have done to this.

MACBETH:                         If we should fail?

LADY MACBETH:                                We fail?
But screw your courage to the sticking-place,          *60*
And we'll not fail. When Duncan is asleep
(Whereto the rather shall his day's hard journey
Soundly invite him) his two chamberlains
Will I with wine and wassail so convince
That memory, the warder of the brain,                  *65*
Shall be a fume, and the receipt of reason
A limbeck only; when in swinish sleep
Their drenched natures lie as in a death,
What cannot you and I perform upon
The unguarded Duncan? what not put upon                *70*
His spongy officers, who shall bear the guilt
Of our great quell?

MACBETH:                         Bring forth men-children only!
For thy undaunted mettle should compose

74 *received* accepted as true.

72–7 Her confidence and the plausibility of her plan transform his attitude to the murder.

77 *other* otherwise.

79 *bend up*, like a bow being prepared for shooting. He takes up the metaphor from line 60.

80 *corporal agent* bodily power.

81 *mock the time* delude the world.

82 He has learnt from her that 'to alter favour ever is to fear' (1.5.71), but he speaks regretfully.

Why is this scene considered crucial? Have your opinions of the characters changed in the course of it? Do people in real life influence each other as this wife influences her husband?

Nothing but males. Will it not be received,
When we have marked with blood those sleepy two          75
Of his own chamber and used their very daggers,
That they have done't?

LADY MACBETH:                Who dares receive it other,
As we shall make our griefs and clamour roar
Upon his death?

MACBETH:              I am settled, and bend up
Each corporal agent to this terrible feat.               80
Away, and mock the time with fairest show:
False face must hide what the false heart doth know.

                                          [*Exeunt.*

### A courtyard in the castle

1 *How goes the night*   what is the time of night?

4 *husbandry*   thrift.

5 *Their candles are all out.*   The stars have hidden their fires:
Macbeth's command at 1.4.50 seems to have been obeyed.
Many of the stage-effects now created by electricians, Shakespeare achieved by words; his audience in the day-lit Globe had
to imagine darkness for much of *Macbeth*. *Take thee that too.*
Banquo hands Fleance a cloak, helmet or belt. Father and son
are on their way to bed, after leaving the King; Banquo is now
off duty.

6 *heavy summons*   deep tiredness.

7 *would not*   do not want to. He dreads nightmares; as he shows
in line 20, the witches haunt his dreams. *powers*   special angels
responsible for warding off evil spirits.

8 *nature*   human nature.

9 *Give me my sword.*   Banquo's jumpiness, when he sees an ap-
proaching torch, adds to the tension.

14 *largess*   bounty. *offices*   servants' quarters.

15 *withal*   with especially. Macbeth takes, without comment, the
gift for his wife. In Shakespeare's time, the *diamond* was valued
as an amulet against nightmares, witchcraft and possession by
devils.

16 *By the name of*   addressing her as. *shut up*   the King ended the
day. Duncan was characteristically generous, appreciative and
happy as he went unawares to his deathbed.

17-19 *Being unprepared . . . wrought*   because we were unprepared, our aim was thwarted by inadequate provision, or else
we would have entertained liberally.

22 yet, when you and I can find a convenient hour.
23 *would*   should.

# ACT TWO

# SCENE ONE

*Enter* BANQUO, *and* FLEANCE *with a torch before him.*

BANQUO: How goes the night, boy?
FLEANCE: The moon is down; I have not heard the clock.
BANQUO: And she goes down at twelve.
FLEANCE:                  I take't, 'tis later, sir.
BANQUO: Hold, take my sword. There's husbandry in heaven;
   Their candles are all out. Take thee that too.         5
   A heavy summons lies like lead upon me,
   And yet I would not sleep. Merciful powers,
   Restrain in me the cursed thoughts that nature
   Gives way to in repose!

*Enter* MACBETH, *and a Servant with a torch.*

                 Give me my sword—
   Who's there?                                10
MACBETH: A friend.
BANQUO: What, sir, not yet at rest? The king's a-bed:
   He hath been in unusual pleasure, and
   Sent forth great largess to your offices.
   This diamond he greets your wife withal,         15
   By the name of most kind hostess; and shut up
   In measureless content.
MACBETH:              Being unprepared,
   Our will became the servant to defect,
   Which else should free have wrought.
BANQUO:                All's well.
   I dreamt last night of the three Weird Sisters:     20
   To you they have showed some truth. – *digging*
MACBETH:                   I think not of them:
   Yet, when we can entreat an hour to serve,
   We would spend it in some words upon that business,

25 *consent* party; or, advice. Macbeth is being intentionally vague, hinting at his succession to the throne somehow—despite Malcolm—after Duncan's natural death in the remote future. Banquo's reply is, in contrast, unequivocal: he will associate himself with honourable affairs, but with no others.

25-6 *If you shall . . . you* if you will belong to my party, when it comes into being; or, if you will follow my advice when we have our talk.

26 *so* provided that. *none* no honour.

27 *augment it* gain higher status.

28 *bosom franchised* heart free from guilt. *clear* innocent.

29 *I shall be counselled* I shall listen to what you have to say.

31 The ringing of the bell was a prearranged signal; see line 62.

33-4 *Is this a dagger . . . hand?* Unlike the ghost and apparitions later in the play, this vision of a dagger in the air is invisible to us. Macbeth's mind at 1.7.18–28 seemed so overwrought that we are prepared to accept this hallucination.

34 *Come.* Speaking and moving as if in a trance, he tries to touch the vision.

36 *sensible to* perceptible by.

39 *heat-oppressed* feverish.

40 *yet* still. *palpable* feelable.

41 *this.* Macbeth draws his own dagger from its sheath. His hand moves as if under an ominous compulsion, although he naturally desires to compare the illusory dagger with his real one.

42 The visionary dagger points the way to Duncan's door.

44-5 *Mine eyes . . . rest* either my eyes are being fooled by my other senses (notably touch, which cannot feel the dagger) or else my eyes are worth all my other senses.

46 *dudgeon* hilt. *gouts* drops.

47 *There's no such thing.* The vision fades.

48 *informs* takes shape.

49 *one half-world* our hemisphere.

50 *wicked dreams.* He, like Banquo (see lines 7–9), has had nightmares.

51 *curtained,* by eyelids, or by the curtains of a four-poster bed which were closed at night.

52 *Hecate* (the final *e* is silent) goddess of witchcraft. *Pale Hecate's offerings* rituals of pale Hecate, such as those in 4.1.

52-3, *Murder, Alarumed* the personification of murder, aroused to action like a soldier in the night.

If you would grant the time.
BANQUO:                    At your kind'st leisure.
MACBETH: If you shall cleave to my consent, when 'tis,
It shall make honour for you.
BANQUO:                    So I lose none                    26
In seeking to augment it, but still keep
My bosom franchised and allegiance clear,
I shall be counselled.
MACBETH:               Good repose the while!
BANQUO: Thanks, sir: the like to you!                    30

                              [*Exeunt* BANQUO *and* FLEANCE.
MACBETH: Go bid thy mistress, when my drink is ready
She strike upon the bell. Get thee to bed.

                              [*Exit* Servant.

Is this a dagger which I see before me,
The handle toward my hand? Come, let me clutch thee.
I have thee not, and yet I see thee still.                    35
Art thou not, fatal vision, sensible
To feeling as to sight? or art thou but
A dagger of the mind, a false creation,
Proceeding from the heat-oppressed brain?
I see thee yet, in form as palpable                    40
As this which now I draw.
Thou marshall'st me the way that I was going;
And such an instrument I was to use.
Mine eyes are made the fools o'th'other senses,
Or else worth all the rest: I see thee still;                    45
And on thy blade and dudgeon gouts of blood,
Which was not so before. There's no such thing:
It is the bloody business which informs
Thus to mine eyes. Now o'er the one half-world
Nature seems dead, and wicked dreams abuse                    50
The curtained sleep; witchcraft celebrates
Pale Hecate's offerings; and withered Murder,
Alarumed by his sentinel, the wolf,

54 *watch*  watchword, sentinel's call. *thus.* The stealthy movements of the great actors David Garrick and Laurence Olivier
   at this point are famous for their dramatic power.

55 *Tarquin's ravishing strides*  the strides of Tarquin on his way
   to rape Lucretia. Tarquin, King of Rome, abused the hospitality of the virtuous Lucretia in the dead of night by forcing
   her, on pain of death, to yield to his embraces. (Shakespeare had
   used the story, which was well-known, in his narrative poem
   *The Rape of Lucrece*.) What aspects of Macbeth's deed are like
   Tarquin's? The classical allusion adds ghastliness to Macbeth's
   deed because the story of Tarquin is bitterly cruel. Macbeth
   himself tastes the full horror.

58 *prate*  blab. *whereabout*  whereabouts.

59 *take*  extract.

59-60 *And take . . . it.*  Macbeth, with appalled fascination,
   watches the scene as if he were not in it, and he finds a terrible
   aptness in its silence.

62 *I go,*  because the signal calls. *invites;* 'my drink is ready'
   (line 31) but the bell calls for murder.


### The same

The action continues straight on from the previous scene.


2 *fire*  courage. She has been drinking to strengthen her nerve.
   *Hark!* Despite the boldness which Lady Macbeth declares
   liquor has given her, she is startled by a sudden noise.

3 *Peace!*  With relief, she realises that a bird shrieked and not a
   man.

4 The owl's shriek was thought to portend death.

5 *stern'st*  cruellest.

4-5 *the fatal . . . good-night.*  At midnight before an execution in
   London, the bellman would ring a bell outside the condemned
   cell.

5 *He is about it.*  Macbeth is committing the murder.

6 She left the doors open herself. *surfeited grooms* servants,
   grooms of the chamber, who have drunk too much. They sleep
   in the King's room.

7 *charge*  duty as the King's guards. *possets* hot drinks taken
   before sleep.

8 *nature*  life. *contend about*  quarrel over.

9 *Whether*  to decide whether.

1-9 How do her references to sound increase the horror of her
   running-commentary?

Whose howl's his watch, thus with his stealthy pace,
With Tarquin's ravishing strides, toward his design          55
Moves like a ghost. Thou sure and firm-set earth,
Hear not my steps which way they walk, for fear
Thy very stones prate of my whereabout,
And take the present horror from the time,
Which now suits with it. Whiles I threat, he lives:          60
Words to the heat of deeds too cold breath gives.

> [*A bell rings.*

I go, and it is done: the bell invites me.
Hear it not, Duncan, for it is a knell
That summons thee to heaven or to hell.

> [*Exit.*

*Duncan
doomed.*


# SCENE TWO

*Enter* LADY MACBETH.

LADY MACBETH: That which hath made them drunk hath
    made me bold:
What hath quenched them hath given me fire. Hark!
Peace!
It was the owl that shrieked, the fatal bellman,
Which gives the stern'st good-night. He is about it:          5
The doors are open; and the surfeited grooms
Do mock their charge with snores: I have drugged their
    possets,
That death and nature do contend about them,
Whether they live or die.

10 Macbeth thinks he hears a noise, loses control of himself for a moment, and calls from off-stage.

12–13 *the attempt . . . us*  if he has attempted the deed but failed, we are ruined.

13 *Hark!*  She listens intently.

13–15 *I laid . . . done't.*  At 1.5.51 she intended to kill Duncan herself. At 1.7.69 she suggested that she and Macbeth together should kill him. She has, however, gone before her husband to Duncan's room, and prepared the grooms' daggers for Macbeth to use. Did 1.7.54–5 reveal tenderness besides ruthlessness? Have the spirits of darkness, invoked at 1.5.39–49, possessed her utterly?

15 Macbeth enters with two daggers in one blood-stained hand; his other hand also is covered in blood. *My husband!* She speaks with admiration, horror and relief.

17 Crickets, like owls, were thought to foretell death.

18 *Did not you speak?*  She refers scornfully to his cry at line 10.

16–21 With extreme economy of language, Shakespeare creates a stifling atmosphere of guilt and anxiety.

22 *sorry*  pitiable.


The modern theatre, like Shakespeare's, relies on its actors to draw the public, and the leading role in *Macbeth* is extremely taxing. Laurence Olivier's performance at Stratford-upon-Avon in 1955 was one of the greatest in modern times: he evoked horror and pity by most subtle and intense acting. The drawing opposite shows him with Vivien Leigh, his Lady Macbeth.

In that production, scenery was realistic and costumes were archaic in style: the show looked entirely different from those at the Globe Theatre and Whitehall Palace. No doubt the style of acting and the whole interpretation of the play were far from Shakespeare's own: this is inevitable. Every actor and producer has to visualize the play in his own mind, and re-create it for a contemporary audience, not a Jacobean one.

The meaning of the play differs from age to age, and changes of interpretation are mirrored in different styles of production. There is no single 'right' way to present *Macbeth*. That is why the illustrations in this book show various sorts of performance, and the performance that you visualize as you read the play will differ from them all. You, as director of that imaginary performance, must interpret the speeches to reveal character and motive, see the whole drama in your mind's eye and discover what its meaning is for you. As you mature, so will your interpretation of the play alter: the richness of Shakespeare's work is inexhaustible. He was, however, a working dramatist who wrote popular hits for a thriving troupe of players. If you can produce or act in *Macbeth* at your school, you will learn far more about the play than if you let your imagined performance remain unrealized in your mind.

MACBETH: [*Within.*] Who's there? what, ho!                    10
LADY MACBETH: Alack! I am afraid they have awaked,
　And 'tis not done: the attempt and not the deed
　Confounds us. Hark! I laid their daggers ready;
　He could not miss them. Had he not resembled
　My father as he slept, I had done't.

### Enter MACBETH.

　　　　　　　　　　My husband!                    15
MACBETH: I have done the deed. Didst thou not hear a noise?
LADY MACBETH: I heard the owl scream and the crickets cry.
　Did not you speak?
MACBETH:　　　　　When?
LADY MACBETH:　　　　　Now.
MACBETH:　　　　　　　As I descended?
LADY MACBETH: Ay.
MACBETH: Hark!                    20
　Who lies i' the second chamber?
LADY MACBETH:　　　　　Donalbain.
MACBETH: [*Looking at his hand.*] This is a sorry sight.

24 *one* one of the two princes, Malcolm and Donalbain, who shared the second chamber.

26 *addressed them* prepared themselves.

27 *There are two . . . together.* She explains that their waking should not surprise or alarm Macbeth.

29 *As* as if. *hangman* executioner. Lady Macbeth does not yet see the hand which holds the daggers.

30 *Listening* listening to.

33 *I had . . . blessing.* Macbeth knows that he is damned. He described, at 1.7.16–25, his pre-vision of his soul's peril.

35 *it* the obsession. Her warning shows insight.

36 *a voice.* Whose voice was this?

38 *knits . . . sleave* gathers into order the tangled skein of silk.

39 A *bath* refreshes.

40 *course* course of food.

41 *chief nourisher.* The second course at dinner was the meat-course and the most substantial.

24–47 Macbeth, gripped by the memory of his experience, is locked in his own horror. His musings are virtually a soliloquy, which Lady Macbeth witnesses with increasing alarm. Here he is haunted by sounds rather than sights, and the titles in line 43 echo the witches' greeting at 1.3.48–9.

36–44 See the first witch's prophecy, 1.3.19–25.

46 *unbend.* He bent up 'Each corporal agent' at 1.7.79.

48 *witness* evidence. *hand.* He now lifts both hands to look at them, and so enables her for the first time to catch sight of the daggers.

LADY MACBETH: A foolish thought to say a sorry sight.

MACBETH: There's one did laugh in's sleep, and one cried
  'Murder!'
  That they did wake each other: I stood and heard them;
  But they did say their prayers, and addressed them          26
  Again to sleep.

LADY MACBETH: There are two lodged together.

MACBETH: One cried 'God bless us!' and 'Amen' the other:
  As they had seen me with these hangman's hands.
  Listening their fear, I could not say 'Amen'                 30
  When they did say 'God bless us!'

LADY MACBETH:                 Consider it not so deeply.

MACBETH: But wherefore could not I pronounce 'Amen'?
  I had most need of blessing, and 'Amen'
  Stuck in my throat.

LADY MACBETH:       These deeds must not be thought
  After these ways: so, it will make us mad.                   35

MACBETH: Methought I heard a voice cry 'Sleep no more!
  Macbeth does murder sleep'—the innocent sleep,
  Sleep that knits up the ravelled sleave of care,
  The death of each day's life, sore labour's bath,
  Balm of hurt minds, great nature's second course,            40
  Chief nourisher in life's feast,—

LADY MACBETH:                 What do you mean?

MACBETH: Still it cried 'Sleep no more!' to all the house:
  'Glamis hath murdered sleep, and therefore Cawdor
  Shall sleep no more—Macbeth shall sleep no more!'

LADY MACBETH: Who was it that thus cried? Why, worthy
    Thane,                                                     45
  You do unbend your noble strength to think
  So brainsickly of things. Go get some water
  And wash this filthy witness from your hand.
  Why did you bring these daggers from the place?
  They must lie there: go carry them, and smear                50
  The sleepy grooms with blood.

55 *the eye of childhood*   only the eyes of a child.

56 *painted*   picture of the.

54–6 She wants to convince herself that there is nothing to be afraid of. Duncan in death, as in sleep, may resemble her father.

57 *gild*   make golden. Shakespeare often refers to gold as 'red'. Macbeth speaks of Duncan's 'golden blood' (2.3.113): the precious blood of the sovereign is aptly, if fancifully, described as 'golden'. It will enrich the grooms' faces.

58 *guilt*.   She puns on 'gilt' (gold laid on the surface) and 'guilt'. Her grim word-play shows her great strain in going to smear the grooms.

*S.D. Knocking within*.   *within*   off-stage. We do not know what makes this noise, which startles Macbeth like a supernatural summons. But he is more terrified of his hands, which seem to have a separate life of their own, as did the hand, eye and knife at 1.4.52–3 and 1.5.51–3.

60 Macbeth's expression of terror may be an echo of Matthew 18:9, 'And if thine eye cause thee to offend, pluck it out, and cast it from thee: it is better for thee to enter into life with one eye, than having two eyes to be cast into hell fire.'

61 *Neptune*   the Roman god of the sea.

62 *No*.   The word is emphatic with emotion.   *rather*   more likely.

63 *incarnadine*   dye blood-red.

64 *one red*   entirely red.

61–4 The opulent words suggest limitless oceans. Notice the rich contrast between polysyllabic line 63 and monosyllabic 64.

65 She makes him withdraw his gaze from his own hands.

67 *At the south entry*.   She tells us where the noise, which seemed like a supernatural call to judgement, really comes from.

68 But Macbeth knows that not 'all great Neptune's ocean' can cleanse him (line 61).

69 *constancy*   firmness.

70 *Hath left you unattended*   has deserted you.

71 *night-gown*   dressing-gown.

72 *watchers*   still up and dressed.

73 *poorly*   dejectedly.

74 If I am to be fully aware of my deed, I had better not see it as mine (and so I ought to continue to be 'lost' in thought).

75 Is this prayer to the invisible knocker a cry or a murmur? Lady Macbeth, more resourceful than her husband, perhaps takes his hand and leads him off.

MACBETH:                                  I'll go no more:
  I am afraid to think what I have done;
  Look on't again I dare not.

LADY MACBETH:                      Infirm of purpose!
  Give me the daggers. The sleeping and the dead
  Are but as pictures; 'tis the eye of childhood          55
  That fears a painted devil. If he do bleed,
  I'll gild the faces of the grooms withal,
  For it must seem their guilt.

                        *[Exit. Knocking within.*

MACBETH:                          Whence is that knocking?
  How is't with me, when every noise appals me?
  What hands are here! Ha! they pluck out mine eyes.       60
  Will all great Neptune's ocean wash this blood
  Clean from my hand? No; this my hand will rather
  The multitudinous seas incarnadine,
  Making the green one red.

           *Re-enter* LADY MACBETH.

LADY MACBETH: My hands are of your colour; but I shame     65
  To wear a heart so white. [*Knocking within.*] I hear a
    knocking
  At the south entry; retire we to our chamber.
  A little water clears us of this deed:
  How easy is it then! Your constancy
  Hath left you unattended. [*Knocking within.*] Hark! more
    knocking.                                              70
  Get on your nightgown, lest occasion call us
  And show us to be watchers. Be not lost
  So poorly in your thoughts.

MACBETH: To know my deed, 'twere best not know myself.

                        *[Knocking within.*

  Wake Duncan with thy knocking! I would thou couldst!

                           *[Exeunt.*

*The same*

The action and the knocking continue straight on from the previous
scene. Macbeth's awareness of damnation is linked to the porter's
ironic game: but prose helps to change the atmosphere.

The porter has been drinking heavily and has hardly slept since.
He delays unlocking the castle-gate while he wryly pretends that
it is the gate of hell, where he welcomes imaginary sinners.

Comic relief is used by dramatists as a safety-valve for the
audiences' pent-up feelings; but the horribly funny porter, unaware that murder has, indeed, made him guardian of the damned,
increases our sense of doom even while we laugh.

In casting *Macbeth*, which of the two types of porter drawn on
the opposite page would you prefer? The thin one wears a nightcap.

2 *old* plenty of.

4 *Beelzebub.* One of the leading devils, Satan's second-in
command.

4-5 *Here's a farmer . . . plenty.* The farmer hoarded his corn and
hoped for a poor harvest, so that he could sell at a high price:
but the harvest promised to be plentiful, and he therefore des-
paired and hanged himself.

5 *time-server* a man who works according to the seasons; or,
serves his own interests; or, undergoes a term of imprisonment.
The porter puns copiously.

5-6 *have napkins . . . you* bring plenty of handkerchiefs with you,
to mop up your sweat.

6-7 *S.D. Knocking within.* If the porter carries a jug, he possibly
drinks from it now.

7 *the other devil*, whose name the porter has forgotten, is Satan.
(Beelzebub was mentioned at line 4.) *an equivocator* a person
who deliberately uses ambiguous words in order to deceive.

9 *scales* of justice.

8-10 *an equivocator . . . heaven.* Father Garnet was hanged on
3 May, 1606, for complicity in the Gunpowder Plot. At his
trial, two months before, he defended himself by equivocation,
and insisted that he was right to do so. James I attended the
trial incognito, and he and his loyal subjects considered equivocation a damnable offence. It was highly topical when Shakespeare wrote *Macbeth*. Father Garnet used the name 'Farmer',
and so there may be a pun in line 4.

## SCENE THREE

*Knocking within. Enter a Porter.*

PORTER: Here's a knocking indeed! If a man were porter of
hell-gate, he should have old turning the key. [*Knocking
within.*] Knock, knock, knock! Who's there, i'the name of
Beelzebub? Here's a farmer that hanged himself on the
expectation of plenty: come in time-server; have napkins    5
enough about you; here you'll sweat for't. [*Knocking
within.*] Knock, knock! Who's there, i'the other devil's
name? Faith, here's an equivocator, that could swear in
both the scales against either scale; who committed treason
enough for God's sake, yet could not equivocate to heaven:    10

**12-13** *Here's an English . . . hose.* The English tailor, who made up garments from his customers' cloth, habitually skimped his work and stole the material he saved. Now he has again tried his usual trick, but the small quantity of cloth used in tight breeches has exposed his knavery.

**13** *French hose* breeches in the French style. The ample style had just gone out of fashion: tight French hose were in. English tailors, as usual, adopted foreign modes.

**14** *roast your goose* heat your smoothing-iron (which has a handle shaped like a goose's neck); also, 'do for yourself'.

**16** *too cold.* Does he rub his hands, blow on his fingers, flap his arms?

**18** *primrose way . . . bonfire* attractive path to hell.

**19** *Anon, anon!* He calls to those who knock that he is coming quickly. *I pray you . . . porter.* As he lets in Macduff and Lennox, perhaps he asks them for a tip.

**23** *the second cock* about 3 a.m.

**25** *What three . . . provoke?* Macduff, who has mastered any irritation he felt at being kept waiting outside in the early morning, acts as the comedian's 'feed' by asking the expected question. What part had drink played in the murder of Duncan?

**26** *nose-painting* nose-reddening. Tipplers tend to get red noses. *Lechery* lust.

**29** *takes away* weakens.

**30** *equivocator* trickster, double-dealer. (See note on line 8.)

**31** *it sets . . . off* it encourages him and discourages him.

**32-3** *stand to* get ready for action.

**34-5** *equivocates . . . sleep* tricks him into sleeping; also, deludes him by a dream.

**35** *giving . . . lie* laying him out, like a wrestler.

**26-35** Perhaps drink had a similar effect on Lady Macbeth's intention to murder Duncan; by revealing his resemblance to her father, liquor unexpectedly discouraged her.

**37** *the very throat on me* my very throat. 'To lie in one's throat' was to tell a deep lie: the porter is punning.

**39** *took up my legs,* as in wrestling; also, as a dog urinates. *sometime* sometimes.

**39-40** *made a shift* managed. *cast* throw, like a wrestler; also vomit.

**42** Macbeth's dressing-gown and clean hands deceive Macduff.

O, come in, equivocator. [*Knocking within.*] Knock, knock,
knock! Who's there? Faith, here's an English tailor come
hither for stealing out of a French hose: come in, tailor;
here you may roast your goose. [*Knocking within.*] Knock,
knock; never at quiet! What are you? But this place is      15
too cold for hell. I'll devil-porter it no further: I had
thought to have let in some of all professions that go the
primrose way to the everlasting bonfire. [*Knocking within.*]
Anon, anon! [*Opens the gate.*] I pray you, remember the
porter.                                                      20

*Enter* MACDUFF *and* LENNOX.

MACDUFF: Was it so late, friend, ere you went to bed,
   That you do lie so late?
PORTER: Faith, sir, we were carousing till the second cock;
   and drink, sir, is a great provoker of three things.
MACDUFF: What three things does drink especially provoke?   25
PORTER: Marry, sir, nose-painting, sleep, and urine. Lechery,
   sir, it provokes and unprovokes: it provokes the desire,
   but it takes away the performance. Therefore, much drink
   may be said to be an equivocator with lechery: it makes   30
   him, and it mars him; it sets him on, and it takes him off;
   it persuades him, and disheartens him; makes him stand
   to, and not stand to; in conclusion, equivocates him in a
   sleep and, giving him the lie, leaves him.                 35
MACDUFF: I believe drink gave thee the lie last night.
PORTER. That it did, sir, i'the very throat on me; but I
   requited him for his lie; and, I think, being too strong for
   him, though he took up my legs sometime, yet I made a
   shift to cast him.                                         40
MACDUFF: Is thy master stirring?

*Enter* MACBETH.

Our knocking has awaked him; here he comes.
LENNOX: Good morrow, noble sir.
MACBETH:                         Good morrow, both.
MACDUFF: Is the King stirring, worthy Thane?
MACBETH:                                      Not yet.

45 *timely* early.

47 *this* giving hospitality to the King and his retinue.
48 *one* a trouble.
49 *physics pain* acts as a medicine to trouble.

51 *limited service* appointed duty. Macduff had been given the task of calling the King.
52 An echo of the conversation at 1.5.58.

54–63 Cosmic forces were expected, in Shakespeare's day, to be disrupted by the death of monarchs. Disorder in the universe portended chaos in the kingdom. This storm, in which evil spirits upset the order of nature, may have been raised by the witches.

58 *combustion* civil tumult. *confused* disorderly.
59 *new-hatched* newly born. *obscure bird* owl. (Lady Macbeth heard it at 2.2.2.)

61 *shake,* with earthquake.

63 *a fellow* an equal.

64–5 *Tongue . . . thee!* heart cannot conceive and tongue cannot name. Macduff can hardly put words in a coherent order.
66 *confusion* ruin.
67 *sacrilegious.* To kill God's earthly deputy is to violate a sacred person: regicide is therefore sacrilege.
68 *The Lord's anointed temple* the King's body, which houses the spirit of God; also, the forehead from which life has been robbed.
67–8 David referred to Saul as 'the Lord's anointed' (1 Samuel 24: 10) and refused to attack such a sacred person. St Paul called the human body 'the temple of the living God' (2 Corinthians 6: 16). Shakespeare combines the two ideas, and here makes explicit the heinous, sacrilegious nature of Macbeth's deed: until now, its nature has been generally implicit.
72 *Gorgon* object which, like the three snake-haired sisters in Greek myth, turns beholders to stone.

[ 62 ]

MACDUFF: He did command me to call timely on him;     45
  I have almost slipped the hour.
MACBETH:                    I'll bring you to him.
MACDUFF: I know this is a joyful trouble to you;
  But yet 'tis one.
MACBETH: The labour we delight in physics pain.
  This is the door.
MACDUFF:          I'll make so bold to call,     50
  For 'tis my limited service.             [*Exit.*
LENNOX: Goes the King hence to-day?
MACBETH:              He does: he did appoint so.
LENNOX: The night has been unruly: where we lay,
  Our chimneys were blown down; and, as they say,     55
  Lamentings heard i'the air, strange screams of death,
  And—prophesying with accents terrible
  Of dire combustion, and confused events,
  New hatched to the woeful time—the obscure bird
  Clamoured the livelong night: some say the earth     60
  Was feverous and did shake.
MACBETH:               'Twas a rough night.
LENNOX: My young remembrance cannot parallel
  A fellow to it.

*Re-enter* MACDUFF.

MACDUFF: O horror! horror! horror! Tongue nor heart
  Cannot conceive nor name thee!
MACBETH, LENNOX:         What's the matter?     65
MACDUFF: Confusion now hath made his masterpiece!
  Most sacrilegious murder hath broke ope
  The Lord's anointed temple, and stole thence
  The life o'the building.
MACBETH:            What is't you say? the life?
LENNOX: Mean you his Majesty?     70
MACDUFF: Approach the chamber, and destroy your sight
  With a new Gorgon: do not bid me speak;
  See, and then speak yourselves.
                 [*Exeunt* MACBETH *and* LENNOX.

74 *alarum-bell* great bell of the castle. It begins to toll at the end of Macduff's speech.

76 *counterfeit* imitation.

78 *The great doom's image* a picture of judgement-day.

79 *rise up* as if it were judgement-day, when the dead shall arise in their shrouds. *sprites* spirits.

80 *countenance* face.

82 The bell, which would be rung if the castle were attacked, is now like a trumpet calling soldiers to discuss terms with an enemy.

85 *repetition* narration.

86 would kill her as she heard it.

87-8 *Woe, alas! . . . house.* Do you think that Lady Macbeth utters 'a natural expression from an innocent hostess', as one scholar, G. L. Kittredge, asserts? Or do you agree with another scholar, A. C. Bradley, that she makes a 'mistake in acting'?

88 *Too cruel anywhere.* Banquo either speaks sorrowfully, or else he briskly rebukes Lady Macbeth for heartlessness.

93 *mortality* human life.

94 *toys* trifles.

95 *drawn* broached. *lees* dregs.

96 *left* left for. *vault* cellar; also, earth, vaulted by the roof of the heavens; and, crypt.

91-6 In this hypocritical public speech, Macbeth unconsciously sums up his private sense of guilt.

                              Awake! awake!
Ring the alarum-bell. Murder and treason!
Banquo and Donalbain! Malcolm! awake!                    75
Shake off this downy sleep, death's counterfeit,
And look on death itself! up, up, and see
The great doom's image! Malcolm! Banquo!
As from your graves rise up, and walk like sprites,
To countenance this horror!                [*Bell rings.*   80

                *Enter* LADY MACBETH.

LADY MACBETH: What's the business,
   That such a hideous trumpet calls to parley
   The sleepers of the house? speak, speak!
MACDUFF:                              O gentle lady!
   'Tis not for you to hear what I can speak:
   The repetition in a woman's ear                        85
   Would murder as it fell.

                *Enter* BANQUO.

                        O Banquo! Banquo!
   Our royal master's murdered!
LADY MACBETH:                 Woe, alas!
   What, in our house?   - strikes Banquo as odd
BANQUO:               Too cruel anywhere.
   Dear Duff, I prithee contradict thyself,
   And say it is not so.                                  90

           *Re-enter* MACBETH *and* LENNOX.

MACBETH: Had I but died an hour before this chance
   I had lived a blessed time; for, from this instant,
   There's nothing serious in mortality:
   All is but toys; renown and grace is dead,
   The wine of life is drawn, and the mere lees           95
   Is left this vault to brag of.

           *Enter* MALCOLM *and* DONALBAIN.

                    [ 65 ]

100 *O! by whom?* This is spoken very violently.

102 *badged* marked, as with a badge worn by retainers to show whom they served.

104 *stared . . . distracted.* They were aroused from their drugged sleep.

106 *fury* frenzy.

107 A brief, horrified silence may follow Macbeth's announcement that he has just stabbed the grooms. His speech of explanation, 109–18, is full of images, but they stand stiffly apart without blending into subtle poetry.

110 *expedition* haste.

111 *pauser* deliberator.

112 *laced* ornamented, like a rich garment. *golden blood.* See Lady Macbeth's pun on 'gild' and 'guilt' at 2.2.57–8.

113 *nature* life.

114 *ruin* death. *wasteful* destructive.

115 *Steeped* dyed.

116 *Unmannerly breeched* indecently clothed.

118 *make's* make his. *Help me hence, ho!* Lady Macbeth planned, at 1.7.78–9, that she and Macbeth would make their 'griefs and clamours roar' at Duncan's death. Perhaps she has been weeping since line 88, and now, fearing that the strained, elaborate speech of Macbeth may make his hearers suspicious, she tries to divert attention from him by pretending to faint or have hysterics. More probably, she really does collapse.

119 *Look to* look after. Macbeth moves to his wife; perhaps Macduff and Banquo help him to tend her. Donalbain and Malcolm are downstage.

121 *argument* theme.

120–1 *that most . . . ours* we who, as bereaved sons, have most right to make a fuss.

122 *an auger-hole* a tiny hole, made by a carpenter's boring-tool.

124 *brewed* prepared for pouring out, like the false tears of Macbeth and Lady Macbeth.

125 *Upon the foot of motion* ready for expression. *Look to the lady.* Lady Macbeth has apparently fainted. Banquo either calls attendants to carry her off, or tells other characters to clear the way for her.

DONALBAIN: What is amiss?

MACBETH:                               You are, and do not know't:
  The spring, the head, the fountain of your blood
  Is stopped—the very source of it is stopped.

MACDUFF: Your royal father's murdered.

MALCOLM:                              O! by whom? - *clinical*                    100

LENNOX: Those of his chamber, <u>as it seemed,</u> had done't:
  Their hands and faces were all badged with blood;
  So were their daggers, which unwiped we found
  Upon their pillows:
  They stared and were distracted; no man's life        105
  Was to be trusted with them.

MACBETH: O, yet I do repent me of my fury
  That I did kill them.

MACDUFF:                    Wherefore did you so?

MACBETH: Who can be wise, amazed, temperate and furious,
  Loyal and neutral, in a moment? No man:              110
  The expedition of my violent love
  Outran the pauser, reason. Here lay Duncan,
  His silver skin laced with his golden blood;
  And his gashed stabs looked like a breach in nature
  For ruin's wasteful entrance: there, the murderers,
  Steeped in the colours of their trade, their daggers  115
  Unmannerly breeched with gore: who could refrain,
  That had a heart to love, and in that heart
  Courage to make's love known?

LADY MACBETH:                           Help me hence, ho!

MACDUFF: Look to the lady.

MALCOLM: [*Aside to* DONALBAIN.] Why do we hold our
    tongues, that most may claim                        120
  This argument for ours?

DONALBAIN: [*Aside to* MALCOLM.] What should be spoken
  Here, where our fate, hid in an auger-hole,
  May rush and seize us? Let's away
  Our tears are not yet brewed.

MALCOLM: [*Aside to* DONALBAIN.] Nor our strong sorrow
  Upon the foot of motion.

125–32 Banquo takes charge and boldly swears his allegiance to the cause of right.

126 *naked frailties.* Only Macduff and Lennox are fully dressed.

128 *question* discuss.

129 *scruples* doubts.

131 *undivulged pretence* hidden intention.

133 *briefly* quickly.

140 *in men's smiles.* Macbeth may have put on a smile of encouragement at lines 133–4. *near* nearer.

140–1 *the near . . . bloody* the more closely we are related to the villain, the more likely he is to stab us.

144 *dainty of leave-taking* particular about saying good-bye.

145 *shift* slip. *warrant in* justification for.

146 *steals* robs; also, creeps off. The rhyming couplet ends the scene decisively, and the brothers prudently flee.

### Outside the castle

By their commentary in lines 1–20, the old man and Ross add to the description of alarming events which young Lennox gave at 2.3.54–63. The Old Man speaks as the anonymous representative of the common people. These static speeches do not advance the plot but they show the repercussions of it and provide some respite in the intense drama. The scene is, in a sense, choric. Perhaps Ross carries a lantern to overcome the gloom of the sun's eclipse.

3 *sore* dreadful.

4 *Hath trifled former knowings* has made my former experiences seem trifling.

BANQUO:                    Look to the lady . . .          *125*
                    [LADY MACBETH *is carried out.*
And when we have our naked frailties hid,
That suffer in exposure, let us meet,
And question this most bloody piece of work,
To know it further. Fears and scruples shake us:
In the great hand of God I stand, and thence          *130*
Against the undivulged pretence I fight
Of treasonous malice.
MACDUFF:                    And so do I.
ALL:                              So all.
MACBETH: Let's briefly put on manly readiness,
And meet i'the hall together.
ALL:                              Well contented.
                    [*Exeunt all but* MALCOLM *and* DONALBAIN.
MALCOLM: What will you do? Let's not consort with them: *135*
To show an unfelt sorrow is an office
Which the false man does easy. I'll to England.
DONALBAIN: To Ireland, I: our separated fortune
Shall keep us both the safer. Where we are,
There's daggers in men's smiles; the near in blood,   *140*
The nearer bloody.
MALCOLM:                    This murderous shaft that's shot
Hath not yet lighted, and our safest way
Is to avoid the aim: therefore, to horse;
And let us not be dainty of leave-taking,
But shift away: there's warrant in that theft          *145*
Which steals itself when there's no mercy left.    [*Exeunt.*


## SCENE FOUR

*Enter* ROSS *with an* Old Man.

OLD MAN: Threescore and ten I can remember well,
Within the volume of which time I have seen
Hours dreadful and things strange; but this sore night
Hath trifled former knowings.

4 *father*. Ross uses a normal form of address to a much older man.

5 *the heavens* the sky, which is unnaturally dark. 'The heavens' was the name given to the roof which canopied the open-air stage. Its underside, painted with such emblems of the sky as signs of the zodiac and stars, may have been hung with black when tragedies were performed.

6 *his bloody stage* the earth, scene of bloodshed. The Crucifixion was accompanied by earthquake and eclipse, and so is the murder of God's anointed deputy in the kingdom.

7 *lamp* sun.

8 *predominance* superior influence. This term is used in astrology, the study of heavenly bodies' influence on human affairs. *the day's shame* day being ashamed to face the murder.

9-10 *darkness does . . . it* there is darkness in the daytime.

12 *towering* flying very high. *pride of place* highest pitch before stooping on her quarry. The old man uses falconers' terms.

13 *a mousing owl*, which normally hunts close to the ground.

15 *minions of their race* choicest thoroughbreds.

16 *Turned wild in nature* became wild beasts.

11-18 The natural order of bird life is upset, and tame animals not only turn wild but indulge in unnatural cannibalism. See note on 2.3.54-63.

21 *How goes . . . now?* Macduff brings the latest news from the meeting which was arranged at 2.3.133-4: Shakespeare uses him to sketch in some more of the plot. Ross and Macduff probably stand away from the old man.

24 *pretend* aim at. *suborned* bribed.

27 *'Gainst nature still!* always unnatural (as everything seems to be now)!

28 *ravin* devour.

29 *means* source. *Thine own life's means* your father.

30 *will fall upon,* by election.

ROSS:                                 Ah, good father,
  Thou seest, the heavens, as troubled with man's act,                    5
  Threatens his bloody stage: by the clock 'tis day,
  And yet dark night strangles the travelling lamp.
  Is't night's predominance, or the day's shame,
  That darkness does the face of earth entomb,
  When living light should kiss it?
OLD MAN:                         'Tis unnatural,                           10
  Even like the deed that's done. On Tuesday last,
  A falcon, towering in her pride of place,
  Was by a mousing owl hawked at and killed.
ROSS: And Duncan's horses—a thing most strange and
    certain—
  Beauteous and swift, the minions of their race,                         15
  Turned wild in nature, broke their stalls, flung out,
  Contending 'gainst obedience, as they would
  Make war with mankind.
OLD MAN:                     'Tis said they ate each other.
ROSS: They did so, to the amazement of mine eyes,
  That looked upon't.

                        *Enter* MACDUFF.

                        Here comes the good Macduff.    20
  How goes the world, sir, now?
MACDUFF:                         Why, see you not?
ROSS: Is't known who did this more than bloody deed?
MACDUFF: Those that Macbeth hath slain.
ROSS:                                 Alas, the day!
  What good could they pretend?
MACDUFF:                         They were suborned.
  Malcolm and Donalbain, the King's two sons,                             25
  Are stolen away and fled, which puts upon them
  Suspicion of the deed.
ROSS:                     'Gainst nature still!
  Thriftless ambition, that wilt ravin up
  Thine own life's means! Then 'tis most like
  The sovereignty will fall upon Macbeth.                                 30

31 *named* appointed king. *Scone*, where Scotland's kings were customarily crowned.

33 *Colmekill* Iona, the royal burial ground.

36 *Fife*. Macduff is going home to his castle. *thither* to Scone. Ross is going to Macbeth's coronation.

38 lest the old reign prove to have been more comfortable for Scotland than the new reign. Macduff now declares his anxiety, which was suggested by the clipped way he delivered his news to Ross.

40 *benison* blessing.

41 *of* out of.

40-1 The old man implies that Ross is one of those who want to settle the kingdom.

Is Macduff emerging as a distinct character? What qualities has he shown?

MACDUFF: He is already named, and gone to Scone
  To be invested.

ROSS:               Where is Duncan's body?

MACDUFF: Carried to Colmekill,
  The sacred storehouse of his predecessors
  And guardian of their bones.

ROSS:                  <u>Will you to Scone?</u>      35

MACDUFF: <u>No, cousin, I'll to Fife.</u>

ROSS:                 Well, I will thither.

MACDUFF: Well, may you see things well done there: adieu!
  Lest our old robes sit easier than our new!

ROSS: Farewell, father.

OLD MAN: God's benison go with you; and with those     40
  That would make good of bad, and friends of foes!

                                 [*Exeunt.*

*Macbeth only one with gumption not to attend ~~these~~ coronation.*

### In the palace at Forres

Macbeth is now established as king in the palace where, at 1.4,
Duncan ruled. This can be shown by a throne, properties and royal
heraldic devices. After the static previous scene, Shakespeare swiftly
establishes dramatic interest through the uneasy relationship of
Banquo and Macbeth.

4 *It* the succession.

6 *them* the weird women.

7 *shine* show favour.

8 *verities* truths.

10 *But hush, no more.* Has Banquo been tempted, since 2.3.129–32,
by his memory of the witches? Suspecting Macbeth of murder,
he assumes that the prophecy for himself can be fulfilled only
by evil deeds, and so he dismisses ambition.

8–10 In Holinshed's history, Banquo is Macbeth's accomplice, but
James I would dislike seeing his ancestor portrayed on the
stage as a regicide. Subjects should certainly, according to
James I, support their king, however evil, because the monarch
is always God's deputy on earth.

S.D. *Sennet* a trumpet-call, different from a flourish, announcing
a ceremonial entry. Macbeth and his queen are robed and
crowned.

11–18 Macbeth wants the whole court to notice his apparently
benevolent interest in Banquo: the lines are spoken publicly.

11–14 *guest . . . feast . . . supper.* We are reminded of Duncan's
fate when he accepted the Macbeths' hospitality.

13 *all-thing* altogether.

14 *solemn* formal.

15 *I'll.* Macbeth makes the invitation personal by not using the
royal plural.

16 *command,* as opposed to request. *the which* your command.

15–18 These correct sentiments of a loyal subject are disquieting
after lines 2–3. The mutual, hidden distrust of Macbeth and
Banquo gives their dialogue tension.

19, 24, 36 Macbeth asks his sinister questions casually and
privately. Banquo, unaware of their dire significance, replies
without hesitation.

22 which has always been weighty and profitable. Macbeth flatters
Banquo.

23 *we'll take to-morrow* we can make do with it tomorrow.

# ACT THREE

## SCENE ONE

*Enter* BANQUO.

BANQUO: <u>Thou hast it now: King, Cawdor, Glamis, all,</u>
<u>As the weird women promised; and I fear</u>
<u>Thou play'dst most foully for't;</u> yet it was said
It should not stand in thy posterity,
But that myself should be the root and father                    5
Of many kings. If there come truth from them—
As upon thee, Macbeth, their speeches shine—
Why, by the verities on thee made good,
May they not be my oracles as well,
And set me up in hope? But hush, no more.                         10

*Sennet sounded. Enter* MACBETH, *as King*; LADY MACBETH
*as Queen;* LENNOX, ROSS, Lords, Ladies *and* Attendants.

MACBETH: Here's our chief guest.
LADY MACBETH:                          If he had been forgotten,
It had been as a gap in our great feast,
And all-thing unbecoming.
MACBETH: Tonight we hold a solemn supper, sir,
And I'll request your presence.
BANQUO:                          Let your Highness                15
Command upon me; to the which my duties
Are with a most indissoluble tie
For ever knit.
MACBETH: <u>Ride you this afternoon?</u>
BANQUO: <u>Ay, my good lord.</u>                                   20
MACBETH: We should have else desired your good advice—
Which still hath been both grave and prosperous—
In this day's council; but we'll take tomorrow.
Is't far you ride?
BANQUO: <u>As far, my lord, as will fill up the time</u>           25

[ 75 ]

26 *this* now. *go not . . . better* if my horse does not go fast enough.

30 *bestowed* lodged.

30-3 *We hear . . . invention.* Time has passed, and Malcolm and Donalbain have been openly spreading their suspicions of Macbeth.

32 *parricide* murder of their father.

34-5 *cause of . . . jointly* state affairs needing our joint attention.

35 *Hie you* hurry.

37 *our time . . . us* it's time we went.

38-40 Now that Macbeth has elicited all the information he needs, he dismisses his doomed victim with elegant courtesy.

41 Macbeth gestures to include all the court in his command.

42 *society* our presence.

43 *The sweeter welcome* the more to be welcomed.

44 *while* until. *God be with you* goodbye.

11-44 Since he became king, has Macbeth gained confidence, diplomatic guile, a commanding air?

45 *Sirrah.* A term used in addressing an inferior.

48 As soon as he is alone, Macbeth drops his regal manner: the contrast between his public performance and his private character is highly dramatic.

48-72 In this soliloquy, which he probably speaks from the throne, Macbeth presents: 48-9 insecurity; 49-57 mistrust of Banquo's superior character; 57-64 the prospect of Banquo's descendants gaining the throne; 64-70 the price of killing Duncan merely for their benefit; 71-2 determination to intervene.

48-9 *thus is . . . thus* enthroned is nothing without being safely enthroned.

50 *Stick* like daggers. *royalty of nature.* This kingly quality, which Holinshed's Banquo certainly lacked, is perhaps Shakespeare's tribute to James I's ancestor as well as a dramatic device to expose Macbeth.

51 *would* desires to be.

52 *to* in addition.

53 *wisdom* discretion.

49-55 Does Macbeth suspect Banquo of plotting to assassinate him? See 1.7.7-10.


56 *genius is rebuked* guardian spirit is restrained.

56-7 *it is said . . . Caesar.* Plutarch records a soothsayer's remark that Mark Antony's good angel fears that of Octavius Caesar, great-nephew and adopted son of Julius Caesar. *chid* reproached.

'Twixt this and supper; go not my horse the better,
I must become a borrower of the night
For a dark hour or twain.

MACBETH:                                  Fail not our feast.

BANQUO: My lord, I will not.

MACBETH: We hear our bloody cousins are bestowed          *30*
In England and in Ireland, not confessing
Their cruel parricide, filling their hearers
With strange invention; but of that tomorrow,
When therewithal we shall have cause of state
Craving us jointly. Hie you to horse; adieu,             *35*
Till you return at night. Goes Fleance with you?

BANQUO: Ay, my good lord: our time does call upon's.

MACBETH: I wish your horses swift and sure of foot;
And so I do commend you to their backs.
Farewell.                                   [*Exit* BANQUO.
Let every man be master of his time                      *41*
Till seven at night; to make society
The sweeter welcome, we will keep ourself
Till supper-time alone; while then, God be with you!
            [*Exeunt all but* MACBETH *and a* Servant.

Sirrah, a word with you: attend those men                *45*
Our pleasure?

SERVANT: They are, my lord, without the palace gate.

MACBETH: Bring them before us. [*Exit* SERVANT.] To be thus
    is nothing,
But to be safely thus. Our fears in Banquo
Stick deep, and in his royalty of nature                 *50*
Reigns that which would be feared: 'tis much he dares,
And, to that dauntless temper of his mind,
He hath a wisdom that doth guide his valour
To act in safety. There is none but he
Whose being I do fear; and under him                     *55*
My genius is rebuked, as it is said
Mark Antony's was by Caesar. He chid the Sisters
When first they put the name of King upon me,
And bade them speak to him; then, prophet-like,

57-64 Shakespeare's contemporaries, who had greatly feared Queen Elizabeth I's childless death, were acutely aware of the need for a monarch to provide direct heirs. Macbeth will have failed as a king and as a man if he has no son to succeed him.

63 *with* by. *unlineal* unhereditary.

65 *filed* defiled.

67 *rancours* malice. *vessel* cup. Macbeth drank of the 'poisoned chalice' (1.7.11).
68 *jewel* soul.
69 *common enemy of man* devil.
71 *list* scene of contest.
72 *champion* challenge. *the utterance* a fight to the death.
S.D. The murderers seem to be soldiers frustrated in their careers.

78 *under fortune* below what you deserve.
79 *made good* demonstrated.
80 *passed in probation* proved.
81 *borne in hand* deluded. *crossed* thwarted. *instruments* means.
82 *wrought with* used.
83 *notion* mind.
83-4 convince even a half-witted imbecile that this was Banquo's doing.
86 *our point of* the point of our.
88 *this* what Banquo has done. *gospelled* pious. Although Macbeth is conscious of his own damnation, he does not scruple to corrupt the soldiers.
89 *To pray . . . man,* as we are commanded in Matthew 5: 44: 'pray for them which hurt you, and persecute you'. (This translation is from the Geneva Bible: perhaps it influenced Shakespeare more at this point than the Bishops' Bible, which he also used.) Macbeth is being sarcastic but he showed, at lines 50-1, that he is aware of Banquo's kingly goodness, and fears it.
91 *yours* your issue.

They hailed him father to a line of kings.      60
Upon my head they placed a fruitless crown,
And put a barren sceptre in my gripe,
Thence to be wrenched with an unlineal hand,
No son of mine succeeding. If't be so,
For Banquo's issue have I filed my mind;      65
For them the gracious Duncan have I murdered;
Put rancours in the vessel of my peace
Only for them, and mine eternal jewel
Given to the common enemy of man
To make them kings—the seed of Banquo kings!      70
Rather than so, come, Fate, into the list,
And champion me to the utterance! Who's there?

    *Re-enter* Servant, *with two* Murderers.

Now go to the door, and stay there till we call.
                        [*Exit* Servant.
Was it not yesterday we spoke together?
FIRST MURDERER: It was, so please your Highness.
MACBETH:                       Well then, now
Have you considered of my speeches?—know      76
That it was he in the times past which held you
So under fortune, which you thought had been
Our innocent self? This I made good to you
In our last conference; passed in probation with you,      80
How you were borne in hand, how crossed, the instruments,
Who wrought with them, and all things else that might
To half a soul and to a notion crazed
Say 'Thus did Banquo.'
FIRST MURDERER:             You made it known to us.
MACBETH: I did so; and went further, which is now      85
Our point of second meeting. Do you find
Your patience so predominant in your nature
That you can let this go? Are you so gospelled
To pray for this good man and for his issue,
Whose heavy hand hath bowed you to the grave      90
And beggared yours for ever?

JEALOUSY

91 *We are men*. Macbeth, who dared 'do all that may become a man' at 1.7.46, and was then taunted for unmanliness, now treats his tool's protestation with scorn.

92 *catalogue* list.

93–101 Macbeth proceeds, by an elaborate recital of different sorts of dogs, to show that men have different functions in the orderly realm. In tempting the soldiers to become assassins, Macbeth is corrupting the order of the human world.

94 *shoughs* (pronounced *shocks*) shaggy dogs. *water-rugs* rough water-dogs. *demi-wolves* cross-breeds. *clept* called.

95 *valued file* graded list.

97 *housekeeper* watch-dog.

99 *closed* set, like a jewel.

100 *Particular addition* a distinguishing quality.

100–1 *bill that . . . alike* catalogue that calls them all 'dogs'.

102 *station* place. *file* list; also, line of soldiers.

103 *worst rank*. But what title is worse than 'assassin'? *say* prove (by doing what I want).

105 *execution* doing; also, killing. *takes your enemy off*. Macbeth is luring them to 'deep damnation' (1.7.20).

107 *in his life* while he lives.

108 *were perfect* would be in perfect health.

112 *tugged with* hauled about by.

113 *set* stake.

114 *mend* improve.

116 *distance* extent.

117 *being* life. *thrust*, like a sword. The metaphor is suitable for soldiers and murderers.

118 *near'st of life* heart.

119 *barefaced* undisguised.

120 *avouch* authorize. *bid my . . . it* declare that he is being removed simply because I wish it.

121 *For* because of.

122 *wail* must bewail.

123 *thence* that is why.

FIRST MURDERER: We are men, my liege.

MACBETH: Ay, in the catalogue ye go for men;
As hounds and greyhounds, mongrels, spaniels, curs,
Shoughs, water-rugs, and demi-wolves, are clept
All by the name of dogs: the valued file                               95
Distinguishes the swift, the slow, the subtle,
The housekeeper, the hunter, every one
According to the gift which bounteous nature
Hath in him closed; whereby he does receive
Particular addition, from the bill                                     100
That writes them all alike: and so of men.
Now, if you have a station in the file,
Not i'the worst rank of manhood, say it;
And I will put that business in your bosoms
Whose execution takes your enemy off,                                  105
Grapples you to the heart and love of us,
Who wear our health but sickly in his life,
Which in his death were perfect.

SECOND MURDERER: I am one, my liege,
Whom the vile blows and buffets of the world
Have so incensed that I am reckless what                               110
I do to spite the world.

FIRST MURDERER: And I another,
So weary with disasters, tugged with fortune,
That I would set my life on any chance,
To mend it or be rid on't.

MACBETH: Both of you
Know Banquo was your enemy.

SECOND MURDERER: True, my lord.                                        115

MACBETH: So is he mine; and in such bloody distance
That every minute of his being thrusts
Against my near'st of life: and though I could
With bare-faced power sweep him from my sight
And bid my will avouch it, yet I must not,                             120
For certain friends that are both his and mine,
Whose loves I may not drop, but wail his fall
Whom I myself struck down. And thence it is

125 *common* public.

116–26 Macbeth possibly strides to and fro delivering this speech; or perhaps he draws the murderers into a sinister huddle. He could use the movements of his robes, during the interview, to heighten his air of urgency and authority.

128 Macbeth is too impatient to listen to protestations of zest for murder.

130 send someone to tell you precisely the ideal time.

131 *on't* of the murder.

132 *something* some distance. *always thought* you must always remember.

133 *I ... clearness* I need to be kept clear of suspicion.

134 *rubs* roughnesses. *botches* blemishes. The murderers must do their job thoroughly.

138 *Resolve yourselves apart* go and make up your minds.

140 *I'll call ... straight* I'll join you straight away.

141–2 If Macbeth is a harder, more desperate, more terrifying character than he was at 2.1.63–4, why has he become so?

*Another room in the palace*

1 Does she suspect that Macbeth has arranged Banquo's murder?

4 Her feelings are like Macbeth's at 3.1.48–9.

5 when we have got what we desired but no contentment follows.

6 *that which we destroy* our dead victim.

That I to your assistance do make love,
Masking the business from the common eye                    *125*
For sundry weighty reasons.

SECOND MURDERER:                    We shall, my lord,
Perform what you command us.

FIRST MURDERER:                    Though our lives—

MACBETH: Your spirits shine through you. Within this hour
   at most
I will advise you where to plant yourselves,
Acquaint you with the perfect spy o'the time,              *130*
The moment on't; for't must be done tonight,
And something from the palace; always thought
That I require a clearness: and with him—
To leave no rubs nor botches in the work—
Fleance his son, that keeps him company,                   *135*
Whose absence is no less material to me
Than is his father's, must embrace the fate
Of that dark hour. Resolve yourselves apart;
I'll come to you anon.

SECOND MURDERER:        We are resolved, my lord.

MACBETH: I'll call upon you straight: abide within.

                                  [*Exeunt* Murderers.
It is concluded: Banquo, thy soul's flight,                *141*
If it find heaven, must find it out tonight.        [*Exit.*

## SCENE TWO

*Enter* LADY MACBETH *and a* Servant.

LADY MACBETH: Is Banquo gone from court?

SERVANT: Ay, madam, but returns again tonight.

LADY MACBETH: Say to the King I would attend his leisure
For a few words.

SERVANT:            Madam, I will.               [*Exit.*

LADY MACBETH:                    Nought's had, all's spent,
Where our desire is got without content:                    *5*
'Tis safer to be that which we destroy

[ 83 ]

**6–7** In this couplet she sums up her disillusionment.

**8** Husband and wife are parted by their guilt: this scene shows their inability to communicate.

**9** *sorriest* saddest.

**10** *using* being familiar with.

**13** *scorched* slashed.

**14** *close* heal.

**15** *her former tooth* her tooth, as dangerous as before she was 'scorched'.

**16** *frame of things disjoint* universe break in pieces.
*both the worlds* heaven and earth.

**17–23** Macbeth has murdered his own sleep; see 2.2.36.

**20** whom we, to secure our peace by satisfying our ambition, have sent to the peace of the grave.

**21** *lie,* as on a torturing rack.

**22** *ecstasy* frenzy.

**27** *sleek o'er* smooth down.

**30** *apply to* be particularly directed towards.

**30–1** Macbeth tries to deceive Lady Macbeth about his plans for murder. The situation in 1.5.55–72 was very different.

**31** *Present him eminence* give him supreme honour, as 'chief guest' (3.1.11).

**32–3** we are unsafe at the moment, so that we must keep our honour washed in these streams of flattery.

**34** *vizards* masks.

**36** Macbeth's soliloquy in 3.1.48–70 showed the torments in his mind.

**38** *copy* lease. *in them . . . eterne* nature has not given them an eternal lease of life.

**39** *There's* in that there is.

Than by destruction dwell in doubtful joy.

*Enter* MACBETH.

How now, my lord! why do you keep alone,
Of sorriest fancies your companions making,
Using those thoughts which should indeed have died          10
With them they think on? Things without all remedy
Should be without regard: what's done is done.

MACBETH: We have scorched the snake, not killed it:
   She'll close and be herself, whilst our poor malice
   Remains in danger of her former tooth.                     15
   But let the frame of things disjoint, both the worlds suffer,
   Ere we will eat our meal in fear, and sleep
   In the affliction of these terrible dreams
   That shake us nightly. Better be with the dead,
   Whom we, to gain our peace, have sent to peace,            20
   Than on the torture of the mind to lie
   In restless ecstasy. Duncan is in his grave;
   After life's fitful fever he sleeps well;
   Treason has done his worst: nor steel, nor poison,
   Malice domestic, foreign levy, nothing                     25
   Can touch him further.

LADY MACBETH:                Come on:
   Gentle my lord, sleek o'er your rugged looks;
   Be bright and jovial among your guests tonight.

MACBETH: So shall I, love; and so, I pray, be you.
   Let your remembrance apply to Banquo;                      30
   Present him eminence, both with eye and tongue—
   Unsafe the while, that we
   Must lave our honours in these flattering streams,
   And make our faces vizards to our hearts,
   Disguising what they are.

LADY MACBETH:                You must leave this.            35

MACBETH: O, full of scorpions is my mind, dear wife!
   Thou know'st that Banquo and his Fleance lives.

LADY MACBETH: But in them nature's copy's not eterne.

MACBETH: There's comfort yet, they are assailable,

40 *jocund*.   This jaunty word sounds horribly incongruous, despite Lady Macbeth's injunction in line 28.

41 *black Hecate*.   Hecate is 'pale' at 2.1.52. She is associated with the pallor of death in that context, and with the darkness of evil in this.

41–4 The darkness in these lines is resonant with the tolling of a death knell.

42 *shard-borne*   carried by its scaly wings.

44 *What's to be done?*   Does she speak with eagerness, timidity, numb horror? To what extent are he and she still attuned to each other?

45 *chuck*   chick; an affectionate, 'jocund' term.

46 *seeling*   blinding. To seel a hawk in training was to sew his eyelids together in preparation for wearing a hood.

46–50 His brutal invocation to night seems to bring darkness in the sombre, ominous poetry of lines 50–3.

47 *scarf up*   blindfold. *tender*   merciful.

49 *that great bond*   the lease of life of Banquo and Fleance.

50–1 *crow*   rook; it is returning to the rookery.

54 Has Macbeth's eagerness for the coming night made her cringe away from him? He draws her to him as they go.

### A lane through the royal park

The third murderer has just delivered the instructions which Macbeth promised at 3.1.130.

2 we need not mistrust the third murderer, since he tells us.

3 *offices*   duties.

4 *To the direction just*   precisely as Macbeth directed. This allays the first murderer's suspicions of the newcomer.

6 *lated*   belated.

7 *timely inn*   inn in time, before darkness is complete.

9 Banquo calls to grooms: they will take the horses on to the palace.

Then be thou jocund: ere the bat hath flown 40
His cloistered flight, ere to black Hecate's summons
The shard-borne beetle with his drowsy hums
Hath rung night's yawning peal, there shall be done
A deed of dreadful note.
LADY MACBETH:　　　　　What's to be done?
MACBETH: Be innocent of the knowledge, dearest chuck, 45
Till thou applaud the deed. . . . Come, seeling night,
Scarf up the tender eye of pitiful day,
And with thy bloody and invisible hand
Cancel and tear to pieces that great bond
Which keeps me pale! Light thickens, and the crow 50
Makes wing to the rooky wood;
Good things of day begin to droop and drowse,
Whiles night's black agents to their preys do rouse.
Thou marvell'st at my words: but hold thee still;
Things bad begun make strong themselves by ill: 55
So, prithee, go with me.　　　　　　　　[*Exeunt.*

## SCENE THREE

*Enter three* Murderers.

FIRST MURDERER: But who did bid thee join us?
THIRD MURDERER:　　　　　　　　　Macbeth.
SECOND MURDERER: He needs not our mistrust, since he
　delivers
Our offices and what we have to do,
To the direction just.
FIRST MURDERER:　　　Then stand with us.
The west yet glimmers with some streaks of day; 5
Now spurs the lated traveller apace
To gain the timely inn, and near approaches
The subject of our watch.
THIRD MURDERER:　　　Hark! I hear horses.
BANQUO: [*Within.*] Give us a light there, ho!
SECOND MURDERER:　　　Then 'tis he: the rest

Banquo's murderers at the Globe Theatre may have entered on the upper level, as shown in this drawing. The second murderer has leaped down to attack, and the third is about to follow.

10 *who are expected.*
11 *go about* go the long way round.
14–15 Rapid whispers.
15 *Stand to't* stand poised to do it.
16 *Let it come down* deliver the rain of blows.
18 Fleance darts away, leaving the murderers in confusion.

### The hall of the palace

Two thrones, a large table and seats are needed. The 'great feast' was mentioned in 3.1.12. and Macbeth's opening words here show that this is a state banquet.

1 *degrees* ranks, and therefore places at table.
1–2 *at first And last* from beginning to end.
3 *society* our guests.

That are within the note of expectation 10
Already are i'the court.

FIRST MURDERER:                    His horses go about.

THIRD MURDERER: Almost a mile; but he does usually—
So all men do—from hence to the palace gate
Make it their walk.

*Enter* BANQUO *and* FLEANCE, *with a torch.*

SECOND MURDERER: A light, a light!

THIRD MURDERER                       'Tis he.

FIRST MURDERER: Stand to't. 15

BANQUO: It will be rain tonight.

FIRST MURDERER:                    Let it come down.

[*The first* Murderer *strikes out the torch, while the others*
*attack* BANQUO.]

BANQUO: O, treachery! Fly, good Fleance, fly, fly, fly!
Thou mayst revenge. O slave!

                         [*Dies.* FLEANCE *escapes.*

THIRD MURDERER: Who did strike out the light?

FIRST MURDERER:                         Was't not the way?

THIRD MURDERER: There's but one down; the son is fled.

SECOND MURDERER:                         We have lost 20
Best half of our affair.

FIRST MURDERER: Well, let's away, and say how much is done.

                                   [*Exeunt.*

## SCENE FOUR

*A banquet prepared. Enter* MACBETH, LADY MACBETH, ROSS,
LENNOX, Lords *and* Attendants.

MACBETH: You know your own degrees, sit down: at first
and last,
The hearty welcome.

LORDS:          Thanks to your majesty.

MACBETH: Ourself will mingle with society
And play the humble host.

5 *keeps her state* remains seated on her throne.
6 we will ask her to welcome you.

9 The lords show 'their hearts' thanks' by bowing to her.
10 *here*, on a chair in the place of honour at the head of a table.
11 *large* liberal. Macbeth settles his guests and then moves to the murderer lurking in the doorway downstage; they talk unobserved while the party goes on upstage.

14 it is better outside you than inside him.

19 *nonpareil* best of all.

21 *fit* of terror. *perfect* healthy, as Macbeth longed to be at 3.1.107–8.
22 *Whole as the marble* firm as solid marble. *founded* fixed.
23 as free and unrestrained as the surrounding air.
24 *cribbed* shut in a hovel.
25 *saucy* insolent.

27 *trenched* deep-cut.
28 *The least a death to nature* the least enough to kill a man.

29 *worm* serpent. Why does Macbeth think of Banquo and Fleance as snakes?
30 will naturally, in the course of time, produce venom.
31 *tomorrow*, when Macbeth will reward the murderers.
32 *ourselves* one another.
33 *the cheer* encouragement as a host.
33–5 *The feast . . . welcome* a feast is no better than a meal sold for cash, unless the host often declares, during the party, that his guests are welcome.
35 *to feed . . . home* mere feeding is best done at home.

Our hostess keeps her state, but in best time 5
We will require her welcome.

LADY MACBETH: Pronounce it for me, sir, to all our friends;
For my heart speaks they are welcome.

*Enter First* Murderer; *he stands in the door-way.*

MACBETH: See, they encounter thee with their hearts' thanks;
Both sides are even: here I'll sit i'the midst: 10
Be large in mirth; anon, we'll drink a measure
The table round. [*Going to the door.*]
There's blood upon thy face.

MURDERER: 'Tis Banquo's then.

MACBETH: 'Tis better thee without than he within.
Is he dispatched? 15

MURDERER: My lord, his throat is cut; that I did for him.

MACBETH: Thou art the best o'the cut-throats; yet he's good
That did the like for Fleance: if thou didst it,
Thou art the nonpareil.

MURDERER:                   Most royal sir,
Fleance is 'scaped. 20

MACBETH: Then comes my fit again: I had else been perfect;
Whole as the marble, founded as the rock,
As broad and general as the casing air:
But now I am cabined, cribbed, confined, bound in
To saucy doubts and fears. But Banquo's safe? 25

MURDERER: Ay, my good lord: safe in a ditch he bides,
With twenty trenched gashes on his head,
The least a death to nature.

MACBETH:                   Thanks for that.
There the grown serpent lies; the worm that's fled
Hath nature that in time will venom breed, 30
No teeth for the present. Get thee gone; tomorrow
We'll hear, ourselves, again.          [*Exit* Murderer.

LADY MACBETH:                   My royal lord,
You do not give the cheer. The feast is sold
That is not often vouched, while 'tis a-making,
'Tis given with welcome: to feed were best at home; 35

36 *from thence* at a meal away from home.

33–7 Lady Macbeth's elaborate speech suits the public occasion. When has she used this type of diction before?

36–7 *meat, Meeting*. This pun, made in a lighthearted manner, does not carry powerful emotion.

40–1 We would have our most honourable countryman under our roof now if our gracious Banquo were here. Macbeth's gloating compliment summons the ghost who, at the Globe Theatre, probably entered through the trap door: Banquo keeps his word, given at 3.1.29, that he would not fail to appear at the feast. Ghosts were thought to be able to manifest themselves to whom they pleased: no character except Macbeth is able to see Banquo's ghost, and Macbeth has not yet looked in the right direction.

42–3 *Who may . . . mischance.* Macbeth's feigned anxiety is smugly callous.

46 *The table's full.* Macbeth glances at the table, notices that there is no spare place, but does not see who is sitting on the chair which had been empty. *Here*, 'i'the midst', the place which Macbeth 'reserved' at line 10.

49 *done this* killed Banquo. Macbeth wildly addresses his guests, who cannot understand what he is talking about. Then the ghost signs reprovingly towards Macbeth.

50 Macbeth, claiming that he did not himself stab Banquo, speaks to the ghost, who has come to terrify him into self-betrayal.

53–4 *my lord . . . youth.* Her excuse, that Macbeth is liable to fits, comes very promptly. She shows great presence of mind.

53–8 The lords, who got up at Ross's bidding, now sit down again and appear to continue banqueting while Lady Macbeth and Macbeth confer privately.

55 *upon a thought* in a moment.

57 *extend his passion* prolong his fit.

60 *proper stuff!* that's a fine story!

61 *painting* representation, not reality.

62 *air-drawn* imaginary; also, drawn through the air. See 2.1.33–43.

63 *flaws* gusts of passion.

From thence, the sauce to meat is ceremony;
Meeting were bare without it.

MACBETH:                              Sweet remembrancer!
Now good digestion wait on appetite,
And health on both!                              HYPOCRISY

LENNOX:                  May it please your Highness sit? /

MACBETH: Here had we now our country's honour roofed,  ① 40
Were the graced person of our Banquo present;

*The Ghost of* BANQUO *enters, and sits in* MACBETH'S *place.*

Who may I rather challenge for unkindness
Than pity for mischance!

ROSS:                              His absence, sir,
Lays blame upon his promise. Please't your Highness
To grace us with your royal company?                              45

MACBETH: The table's full.

LENNOX:                              Here is a place reserved, sir.

MACBETH: Where?

LENNOX: Here, my good lord. What is't that moves your
  Highness?

MACBETH: Which of you have done this? .

LORDS:                              What, my good lord?

MACBETH: Thou canst not say I did it: never shake          50
  Thy gory locks at me.

ROSS: Gentlemen, rise; his Highness is not well.

LADY MACBETH: Sit, worthy friends: my lord is often thus,
  And hath been from his youth: pray you, keep seat;
  The fit is momentary; upon a thought                              55
  He will again be well. If much you note him,          CHALLENGING
  You shall offend him and extend his passion:          HIS HONOUR.
  Feed, and regard him not. [*Aside.*] Are you a man?

MACBETH: Ay, and a bold one that dare look on that
  Which might appal the devil.

LADY MACBETH:                  O proper stuff!                              60
  This is the very painting of your fear;
  This is the air-drawn dagger which you said
  Led you to Duncan. O, these flaws and starts—

64 *to* compared with. *become* suit.

65 *A woman's story* an old wive's tale.

66 *Authorized* guaranteed. The story-teller says her grand-mother vouched for its truth. *Shame itself!* you are shame personified!

69–70 The ghost gestures before vanishing.

58–68 She tries to taunt him into courage, believing that the ghost (which she cannot see) exists only in his imagination.

71 *charnel-houses* store-houses for bones dug up in making fresh graves.

72 *monuments* tombs.

73 *maws* stomachs.

71–3 if corpses won't stay buried, we had better let birds of prey eat the dead.

75–83 Macbeth is lost in meditation.

76 before human law quietened society and so made it gentle.

78 *The time has been That* but in the old days.

81 *mortal murders* fatal wounds.

83–4 Her taunts of cowardice have not made him master his terror: now she tries reasonable persuasion, speaking aloud so that her guests can hear. He pulls himself together at once.

85 *muse* be amazed.

88 *Then* when I have drunk everybody's health.

91 Once again, the ghost enters at a moment when Macbeth seems, in his ghoulish declaration of goodwill towards Banquo, to be defying the murdered man.

92 *all to all* all good wishes all round. *Our duties . . . pledge* we offer our homage and drink the toast. The lords rise to drink, and Macbeth's frenzy keeps them on their feet, listening and watching.

Impostors to true fear—would well become
A woman's story at a winter's fire,                              65
Authorized by her grandam. Shame itself!
Why do you make such faces? When all's done,
You look but on a stool.

MACBETH: Prithee, see there! behold! look! lo! how say you?
Why, what care I? If thou canst nod, speak too.              70
If charnel-houses and our graves must send
Those that we bury back, our monuments
Shall be the maws of kites.                    [*Exit* Ghost.

LADY MACBETH:                What! quite unmanned in folly?

MACBETH: If I stand here, I saw him.

LADY MACBETH:                         Fie, for shame!

MACBETH: Blood hath been shed ere now, i'the olden time,   75
Ere human statute purged the gentle weal;
Ay, and since too, murders have been performed
Too terrible for the ear. The time has been
That when the brains were out the man would die,
And there an end; but now they rise again,                  80
With twenty mortal murders on their crowns,
And push us from our stools. This is more strange
Than such a murder is.

LADY MACBETH:              My worthy lord,
Your noble friends do lack you.

MACBETH:                        I do forget.
Do not muse at me, my most worthy friends;                  85
I have a strange infirmity, which is nothing
To those that know me. Come, love and health to all;
Then I'll sit down. Give me some wine, fill full.
I drink to the general joy of the whole table,
And to our dear friend Banquo, whom we miss;               90
Would he were here! [*Re-enter* Ghost.] To all, and him,
    we thirst,
And all to all.

LORDS:       Our duties, and the pledge.

In 1613 the thatched Globe Theatre was burnt down, and a new Globe, with a tiled roof, was built instead. The drawing opposite illustrates line 89 in a performance there. The audience was very mixed: it included such diverse people as brilliant law students, solid bakers' wives, stupid carters and frivolous ladies of fashion. London's theatres, famous throughout Europe, provided highly attractive shows. Perhaps 13 per cent of Londoners went to a theatre each week in 1605. At that time—when 3d. would buy the cheapest dinner at an eating house, or a pipeful of tobacco, and when a pint of ale cost 2d.—a penny entrance fee would let you stand in the yard of the Globe, another penny would buy you a seat in the upper gallery, and for a third penny you could have a seat in the lower, better one. If you were willing to pay extra for a chance to display your fashionable clothes, you would buy a more expensive place on the stage itself. You might get a poor view of the play but you would be in the public eye.

The audience, out for a good time, was boisterous and responsive. Actors were not only clapped but hissed too, and their performances matched the plays in full-bloodedness. The repertoire was formidable; every afternoon of the week a different play was put on, and an average run was only 12 performances, spread over as many weeks. A smash hit might achieve 32 performances and a flop two. Theatres were open even in mid-winter, when audiences fell by only a third. During outbreaks of plague, common in summer, the theatres shut (much to the satisfaction of Puritans, who tried to abolish them) and the actors took their plays on tour. Shakespeare's friends and relations at Stratford then got a chance to see *Macbeth*.

The company travelled light, and furniture for the banqueting scene was borrowed locally. On tour, in halls or inn yards, as well as at the Globe Theatre, parts of the stage were strewn with rushes. These protected the costumes of actors who had to fall or lie on the stage. The trap-door, if used for the ghost's entry, was kept clear. An early stage tradition, perhaps dating back to the original production, makes Macbeth drop the cup when he sees the ghost, who may have sat down in the chair behind him while the toast was drunk. There is no food on the Jacobean table in the drawing; dishes were brought round at banquets in Shakespeare's time, and the guests carved for themselves. Even without quantities of food, this scene is difficult to stage.

93 *Avaunt*  go.

95 *speculation*  power of sight.

96–9 Macbeth stands petrified, oblivious of all but the ghost, while Lady Macbeth addresses the lords; and then he continues speaking to the ghost.

99 Macbeth had dared do more: see 1.7.46–51.

100 *like*  in the form of.

101 *armed*  horned. *Hyrcan*  from Hyrcania, a region on the Caspian Sea.

102 *that*  that of Banquo.

104 *to the desert*  to fight in the desert, where there would be no aid.

105 *trembling I inhabit*  stay at home in fear; or, live in terror. *protest*  proclaim.

106 *a baby of a girl*  a baby girl; or, the puny child of an immature mother.

107–8 *Why, so . . . again.*  Macbeth speaks to himself, and then turns to his guests.

107 *Unreal mockery.*  Macbeth persuades himself, for the moment, that he has only imagined the ghost. *being gone*  now that it has gone.

110 *admired*  amazing. *disorder*  lack of self-control.

111 *overcome*  pass over.

112 *You.*  Macbeth refers to Lady Macbeth and to the company in general.

113 *owe*  own.

112–13 *You make . . . owe*  you make me doubt my own nature. (I believed I was brave until now I think of you being unmoved by the sight of the ghost.)

116 *mine*  the natural ruby of my cheeks. Macbeth, deep in thought, moves away from his guests.

118 *At once*  to you all together, not separately in order of precedence.

MACBETH: Avaunt, and quit my sight, let the earth hide thee!
  Thy bones are marrowless, thy blood is cold;
  Thou hast no speculation in those eyes              *95*
  Which thou dost glare with!
LADY MACBETH:            Think of this, good peers,
  But as a thing of custom: 'tis no other;
  Only it spoils the pleasure of the time.
MACBETH: What man dare, I dare:
  Approach thou like the rugged Russian bear,     *100*
  The armed rhinoceros, or the Hyrcan tiger;
  Take any shape but that, and my firm nerves
  Shall never tremble: or be alive again,
  And dare me to the desert with thy sword;
  If trembling I inhabit then, protest me         *105*
  The baby of a girl. Hence, horrible shadow!
  Unreal mockery, hence!            [*Exit* Ghost.
                 Why, so; being gone,
  I am a man again. Pray you, sit still.
LADY MACBETH: You have displaced the mirth, broke the
    good meeting,
  With most admired disorder.
MACBETH:        ·      Can such things be,     *110*
  And overcome us like a summer's cloud,
  Without our special wonder? You make me strange
  Even to the disposition that I owe,
  When now I think you can behold such sights
  And keep the natural ruby of your cheeks,     *115*
  When mine is blanched with fear.
ROSS:               What sights, my lord?
LADY MACBETH: I pray you speak not; he grows worse and
    worse;
  Question enrages him. At once, good night:
  Stand not upon the order of your going,
  But go at once.
LENNOX:        Good night; and better health     *120*
  Attend his Majesty!

121–41 When Lady Macbeth has hustled the alarmed lords away, she sits down listlessly, exhausted by the strain of coping with Macbeth and her guests. He continues meditating and scheming, but she seems numb with weariness.

122–6 Macbeth is lost in gloomy thoughts that 'murder will out'.

122 *It* the murder of Banquo.

123 *stones,* under which the corpse of a murdered man is buried.

124 *Augurs* auguries, from the behaviour and flight of birds.
*understood relations* connections between causes and effects which are apparently unrelated.

125 *maggot-pies* magpies. *choughs* jackdaws.

126 *the night* the time of night. Macbeth rouses himself to ask this question.

127 *at odds with* in conflict with.

128 what do you say to Macduff's refusal to come? She does not seem to know about this. Macbeth is already thinking of his next victim. Key figures in the three distinct but overlapping phases of the play are Duncan, Acts 1 and 2; Banquo, 3.1–3.4; and Macduff, 3.6–end.

127–8 From now on Macduff becomes, symbolically, the bringer of light to the darkened kingdom.

130 *by the way* casually. Macduff is said to have deliberately cut the banquet: but Macbeth, afraid of his disloyalty, will summon him.

131–2 There's not . . . *fee'd.* Macbeth has spies everywhere.

133 *betimes* quickly. The witches must name Macbeth's dangerous enemies; his reckless fear cannot brook delay.

135 *By the worst* even by the worst.

136 *causes* considerations.

137 *more* further.

138 to go back would be as tedious as to go on to the far side.

139 *will to hand* will be done.

140 which must be done before they can be thought about.

141 *season of all natures* power which preserves all life. She shows wifely concern.

142 *we'll to sleep.* The next time she appears, she is sleepwalking. *My strange and self-abuse* my strange self-deception. He still thinks he imagined the ghost.

143 is the beginner's fear which lacks toughening experience.

135–44 Is Macbeth's callous selfishness awe-inspiring, pitiful, amazing, incredible?

LADY MACBETH:       A kind good night to all!
                [*Exeunt* Lords *and* Attendants.

MACBETH: It will have blood; they say, blood will have blood:
Stones have been known to move and trees to speak;
Augurs and understood relations have
By maggot-pies and choughs and rooks brought forth    *125*
The secret'st man of blood. What is the night?

LADY MACBETH: Almost at odds with morning, which is
   which.

MACBETH: How say'st thou, that Macduff denies his person
At our great bidding?

LADY MACBETH:       Did you send to him, sir?

MACBETH: I hear it by the way; but I will send:    *130*
There's not a one of them but in his house
I keep a servant fee'd. I will to-morrow—
And betimes I will—to the Weird Sisters:
More shall they speak; for now I am bent to know,
By the worst means, the worst. For mine own good    *135*
All causes shall give way: I am in blood
Stepped in so far that, should I wade no more,
Returning were as tedious as go o'er.
Strange things I have in head that will to hand,
Which must be acted ere they may be scanned.    *140*

LADY MACBETH: You lack the season of all natures, sleep.

MACBETH: Come, we'll to sleep. My strange and self-abuse
Is the initiate fear that wants hard use:
We are yet but young in deed.           [*Exeunt.*

# Macbeth

## A heath

This scene, 4.1.39–43 and 4.1.125–32 are generally thought not to be by Shakespeare, because they are different in style and effect from the other witch scenes in *Macbeth*. The inferior author is unknown, but he probably wrote his additions to the play after Shakespeare's death in 1616, and certainly before its first publication in 1623. They are cut in modern productions.

The insipid, faintly pretty lines are iambic rhythm and they might be suitable for fairies to speak. Shakespeare's own exciting, grotesque speeches and chants for his witches are in rough trochaic rhythm, generally with a very emphatic beat to start the line, and they are vividly appropriate to the terrible creatures who utter them.

1 *Hecate*, see 2.1.52  *angerly*  angrily.
2 *beldams*  hags.
7 *close contriver*  secret plotter.
11 *wayward son*  fickle devotee of witchcraft.

15 *Acheron*  one of the rivers of hell.  *pit of Acheron*  the witches' cavern, suitably described as a 'pit of hell'.

18 *vessels*,  such as cauldrons.

20 *for the air*  going to fly.
21 *dismal*  disastrous.

24 *vaporous drop*  drop of magic vapour.  *profound*  deeply mysterious.
26 *sleights*  arts.
27 *artificial sprites*  apparitions, visible in 4.1.
28 *illusion*  power to deceive.
29 *confusion*  ruin.

32 *security*  over-confidence.

# SCENE FIVE

*Thunder. Enter the three* Witches, *meeting* HECATE.

FIRST WITCH: Why, how now, Hecate, you look angerly.
HECATE: Have I not reason, beldams as you are,
  Saucy and overbold? How did you dare
  To trade and traffic with Macbeth
  In riddles and affairs of death;                   5
  And I, the mistress of your charms,
  The close contriver of all harms,
  Was never called to bear my part,
  Or show the glory of our art?
  And, which is worse, all you have done       10
  Hath been but for a wayward son,
  Spiteful and wrathful; who, as others do,
  Loves for his own ends, not for you.
  But make amends now: get you gone,
  And at the pit of Acheron                   15
  Meet me i'the morning: thither he
  Will come to know his destiny.
  Your vessels and your spells provide,
  Your charms and everything beside.
  I am for the air; this night I'll spend     20
  Unto a dismal and a fatal end.
  Great business must be wrought ere noon:
  Upon the corner of the moon
  There hangs a vaporous drop profound;
  I'll catch it ere it come to ground:        25
  And that distilled by magic sleights
  Shall raise such artificial sprites
  As by the strength of their illusion
  Shall draw him on to his confusion.
  He shall spurn fate, scorn death, and bear   30
  His hopes 'bove wisdom, grace, and fear;
  And you all know security

33 *S.D. Song within . . . etc.* This song and the one at 4.1.43
   occur in full in *The Witch*, a play of uncertain date by Thomas
   Middleton (1580–1627), but he did not necessarily write the
   rest of this scene. Hecate is a character in *The Witch*.

   Middleton wrote some of his work in collaboration with various
   other playwrights. Co-authorship was then much more common
   in the theatre than it is now, and Shakespeare may have very
   occasionally worked with other dramatists, especially in his
   early days.

34 *spirit* familiar spirit, who appears aloft in an airborne car
   hung with flimsy draperies.

35 *S.D. Exit.* Hecate ascends in the car (which is pulled up by
   concealed ropes), and vanishes through a trap-door in the
   'heavens'.

## Somewhere in Scotland

This is a static scene, comparable to 2.4. It forms a bridge between
past and future, intensifies our feelings and contains many words
that are highly significant in the echoing poetry of *Macbeth*.
*Damned, sleep, heaven, feast, grace, holy, homage, honours, angel,
blessing, prayers* are, for example, all important verbal threads
running through the fabric of this poetic drama.

1 *hit* hinted to.
3 *borne* conducted. *Things have been strangely borne;* this is the
   theme of Lennox's speech, which contains: 3–17, a scornful
   summary of the murders, accusations and hypocrisy of Macbeth;
   17–20, fears and hopes for Malcolm, Donalbain and Fleance;
   21–3, rumours about Macduff. Lennox's tone from 3–20 is
   caustic: he uses irony and sarcasm.
4 *marry* indeed. To pity the dead is easy, but to have let them
   live would be better!
6–7 Citing Fleance's flight as evidence, Macbeth has proclaimed
   him Banquo's murderer: to be out in the dark is dangerous.
8 *cannot want the thought* cannot help thinking. *monstrous* unnatural.
10 *fact* deed.
11 *straight* instantly.
12 *pious* loyal. *delinquents* defaulters: the grooms of the chamber had failed to do their duty.
13 *thralls* prisoners.
14 Lennox did not, at 2.3.101–5, query Macbeth's hacking of the
   grooms. Is Lennox growing less naive? Or is he here not an
   individual character but a mouthpiece for Scotland's disillusioned lords?

Is mortals' chiefest enemy.
> [*Song within, 'Come away, come away,' etc.*

Hark! I am called; my little spirit, see,
Sits in a foggy cloud, and stays for me.                    [*Exit.*    35
FIRST WITCH: Come, let's make haste; she'll soon be back
again.                                                            [*Exeunt.*


# SCENE SIX

*Enter* LENNOX *and another* LORD.

LENNOX: My former speeches have but hit your thoughts,
Which can interpret farther: only I say
Things have been strangely borne. The gracious Duncan
Was pitied of Macbeth: marry, he was dead.
And the right-valiant Banquo walked too late;                       5
Whom, you may say, if't please you, Fleance killed,
For Fleance fled: men must not walk too late.
Who cannot want the thought how monstrous
It was for Malcolm and for Donalbain
To kill their gracious father? Damned fact!                        10
How it did grieve Macbeth! Did he not straight,
In pious rage, the two delinquents tear,
That were the slaves of drink and thralls of sleep?
Was not that nobly done? Ay, and wisely too;
For 'twould have angered any heart alive                           15
To hear the men deny't. So that, I say,

17 *borne.* Lennox picks up the word he used in line 3, and concludes his description of past events with an extremely scornful accent on *well.*

19 *an't* if it. *should* would certainly.

20 *'twere* it would be really like. Macbeth would execute them.

21 *broad* outspoken.

22 *tyrant* usurper; also, despot.

21–3 See 3.4.128–30.

24 *bestows himself* takes refuge.

25 *holds* withholds. *the due of birth* his birthright.

27 by Edward the Confessor with such honour. At its first mention the English court is associated with holiness. The contrast between Edward's Christian kingship and Macbeth's devilish tyranny in Scotland becomes one of the play's main motifs.

29 *his high respect* the high respect in which the rightful king of Scotland is held.

30 *the holy king, upon his aid* Edward, in Malcolm's aid.

31 *wake* arouse to battle. The Earl of Northumberland is later called old Siward. His son, young Siward, is here referred to as 'warlike'—and so he proves to be in Act 5.

34 *meat* food.

35 rid our feasts and banquets of bloody daggers.

36 *faithful* to our rightful king. *free* honestly acquired.

37 *this report* the news from England.

39 *Sent he.* After the banquet: see 3.4.130.

40 *with an absolute 'Sir, not I'* when Macduff flatly refused.

41 the sullen messenger turns his back on him.

42 *hums, as who should say* mutters, as if he were saying. *rue* regret.

43 *clogs* burdens. (Messengers who bring bad news to Macbeth are harshly received at 5.3.11 and 5.5.35.)

44 *him* Macduff.

44–5 *hold what . . . provide* stay as far away as he has sense to.

47 *His* Macduff's.

Has this scene forwarded the action? If so, how and to what extent?

He has borne all things well; and I do think
That had he Duncan's sons under his key—
As, an't please heaven, he shall not—they should find
What 'twere to kill a father; so should Fleance.                    20
But peace! for from broad words, and 'cause he failed
His presence at the tyrant's feast, I hear,
Macduff lives in disgrace. Sir, can you tell
Where he bestows himself?

LORD:                    The son of Duncan,
From whom this tyrant holds the due of birth,                       25
Lives in the English court, and is received
Of the most pious Edward with such grace
That the malevolence of fortune nothing
Takes from his high respect. Thither Macduff
Is gone to pray the holy king upon his aid                          30
To wake Northumberland and war-like Siward,
That by the help of these (with Him above
To ratify the work) we may again
Give to our tables meat, sleep to our nights,
Free from our feasts and banquets bloody knives,                    35
Do faithful homage and receive free honours:
All which we pine for now. And this report
Hath so exasperate the king that he
Prepares for some attempt of war.

LENNOX:                    Sent he to Macduff?

LORD: He did: and with an absolute 'Sir, not I!'                    40
The cloudy messenger turns me his back
And hums, as who should say 'You'll rue the time
That clogs me with this answer.'

LENNOX:                    And that well might
Advise him to a caution to hold what distance
His wisdom can provide. Some holy angel                             45
Fly to the court of England and unfold
His message ere he come, that a swift blessing
May soon return to this our suffering country
Under a hand accursed!

LORD:                    I'll send my prayers with him.
                                        [*Exeunt.*

[ 107 ]

### A cavern, with a boiling cauldron in the middle of it

The witches await the signal to begin casting their spells in preparation for Macbeth's visit, forecast in 3.4.132–3. Smoke and
sound effects can add atmosphere to the scene. Does rhyme give
power to the incantation?

1 *brinded*   brindled, streaked. The cat is 'Graymalkin' of 1.1.8.

2 *hedge-pig*   hedgehog. (Perhaps the second witch has changed
her familiar since 1.1.9.)

3 *Harpier*,   an unknown demon who is the third witch's familiar,
gives the starting-signal.

4–38 As they dance round the cauldron, and throw in the ingredients, perhaps they stir the mixture with their staves.

7–8 has sweated out venom for thirty-one days and nights, and
been captured in its sleep.

10–11 During this refrain and its repetitions, they show by their
movements and gestures that they are increasing the world's
drudgery and wretchedness.

12 slice of snake from the fens.

16 *fork*   forked tongue. *blind-worm*   slow-worm. It was considered venomous.

17 *howlet*   owlet.

23 *Witch's mummy*   medicine prepared from a witch's corpse.
*maw and gulf*   stomach and gullet.

24 *ravined*   glutted (with flesh).

27 *slips of yew*   cuttings of the graveyard tree, which was considered poisonous.

28 *slivered*   sliced off. *eclipse*,   a time of ill-omen.

29 *Turk, Tartar*.   Proverbially cruel and pagan, and therefore
suitable ingredients.

30 *birth-strangled*   strangled at birth and so unbaptized.

# ACT FOUR

## SCENE ONE

*Thunder. Enter the three* Witches.

FIRST WITCH: Thrice the brinded cat hath mewed.

SECOND WITCH: Thrice and once the hedge-pig whined.

THIRD WITCH: Harpier cries; 'tis time, 'tis time.

FIRST WITCH: Round about the cauldron go;
　　　　　　In the poisoned entrails throw.
　　　　　　Toad, that under cold stone
　　　　　　Days and nights has thirty-one
　　　　　　Sweltered venom sleeping got,
　　　　　　Boil thou first i'the charmed pot.　　5

ALL: Double, double toil and trouble;　　10
　　　Fire burn and cauldron bubble.

SECOND WITCH: Fillet of a fenny snake,
　　　　　　In the cauldron boil and bake;
　　　　　　Eye of newt, and toe of frog,
　　　　　　Wool of bat, and tongue of dog,
　　　　　　Adder's fork, and blind-worm's sting,　　15
　　　　　　Lizard's leg, and howlet's wing—
　　　　　　For a charm of powerful trouble,
　　　　　　Like a hell-broth boil and bubble.

ALL: Double, double toil and trouble;　　20
　　　Fire burn and cauldron bubble.

THIRD WITCH: Scale of dragon, tooth of wolf,
　　　　　　Witch's mummy, maw and gulf
　　　　　　Of the ravined salt-sea shark,
　　　　　　Root of hemlock digged i'the dark,　　25
　　　　　　Liver of blaspheming Jew,
　　　　　　Gall of goat, and slips of yew
　　　　　　Slivered in the moon's eclipse,
　　　　　　Nose of Turk, and Tartar's lips,
　　　　　　Finger of birth-strangled babe　　30

31 *ditch-delivered* born in a ditch. *drab* prostitute.

32 *slab* sticky.

33 *chaudron* entrails.

39-43 The stage-directions and lines are not by Shakespeare. See the introduction to 3.5 and note on 3.5.33. Here, 'the other three witches' come to augment the song and dance. There are five or six witches in the similar scene in *The Witch*.

44 Pricking thumbs portended evil.

46-7 The cavern has been charmed against intruders: now the second witch releases the spell. The *locks* are metaphorical.

S.D. Macbeth strides on imperiously: he looks wild, dishevelled and reckless, and he greets the witches with bullying vigour. When he was innocent they came to him; now he comes to them.

48 *black*, because they do black magic.

49 *without a name.* Their secret ritual is too horrible for speech.

50 *conjure* invoke, call upon. *that . . . profess* black magic.

51 *it* your art. He has no scruples about the evil source of the witches' knowledge. See 3.4.135.

52-61 If he can gain his own desires, Macbeth dares to sacrifice the world to complete ruin. In this speech he develops, with violent examples, the idea expressed in 3.2.16.

53 *yesty* foaming.

54 *confound* wreck. *navigation* shipping.

55 *bladed . . . lodged* corn in the blade be blown down flat.

57 *slope* bend down.

59 *Nature's germens* the material and spiritual seeds of life. God's orderly creation may be shattered in atomic disintegration for all Macbeth cares.

60 *sicken* becomes surfeited. The murderer is allied with anarchy.

|   |   |   |
|---|---|---|
| | Ditch-delivered by a drab— | |
| | Make the gruel thick and slab: | |
| | Add thereto a tiger's chaudron, | |
| | For the ingredients of our cauldron. | |
| ALL: | Double, double toil and trouble; | 35 |
| | Fire burn and cauldron bubble. | |
| SECOND WITCH: | Cool it with a baboon's blood, | |
| | Then the charm is firm and good. | |

*Enter* HECATE *and the other three* Witches.

|   |   |   |
|---|---|---|
| HECATE: | O! well done! I commend your pains, | |
| | And every one shall share i'the gains. | 40 |
| | And now about the cauldron sing, | |
| | Like elves and fairies in a ring, | |
| | Enchanting all that you put in. | |

[*Music and a song, 'Black spirits,' etc.*
*Exeunt* HECATE *and the other three* Witches.

|   |   |   |
|---|---|---|
| SECOND WITCH: | By the pricking of my thumbs, | |
| | Something wicked this way comes. | 45 |
| | Open, locks, | |
| | Whoever knocks! | |

*Enter* MACBETH.

MACBETH: How now, you secret, black, and midnight hags!
  What is't you do?
ALL:                 A deed without a name.
MACBETH: I conjure you, by that which you profess—                    50
  Howe'er you come to know it—answer me:
  Though you untie the winds and let them fight
  Against the churches; though the yesty waves
  Confound and swallow navigation up;
  Though bladed corn be lodged and trees blown down;           55
  Though castles topple on their warders' heads;
  Though palaces and pyramids do slope
  Their heads to their foundations; though the treasure
  Of Nature's germens tumble all together,
  Even till destruction sicken—answer me                             60

63 *our masters*, the evil spirits whom the witches serve and who now take the shapes of the Apparitions.

64–7 The second and third witches add these ingredients. ⎯

65 *nine farrow* mystic number of piglets. *sweaten* sweated.

67 *high or low* wherever you are.

68 *office* thy function.
*S.D.* The first apparition is Macbeth's helmeted head.

74 *harped* touched.

76 *More potent*. Macbeth's head will, in fact, fall because of Macduff's bloody birth.
*S.D.* The second apparition is the infant Macduff, ripped from his mother's womb.

78 *three ears*, one for each call.

80 *none of woman born*. Macbeth does not suspect that there may be an equivocation in this phrase. Can a child, cut prematurely from his mother's womb by a violent Caesarean operation, be truly said to be born? Macbeth only thinks of the child as born in the course of nature.

To what I ask you.

FIRST WITCH:     Speak.

SECOND WITCH:     Demand.

THIRD WITCH:       We'll answer.

FIRST WITCH: Say if thou'dst rather hear it from our mouths,
 Or from our masters?

MACBETH:     Call 'em: let me see 'em.

FIRST WITCH:  Pour in sow's blood, that hath eaten
  Her nine farrow; grease that's sweaten   65
  From the murderer's gibbet throw
  Into the flame.

ALL:      Come, high or low;
  Thyself and office deftly show.

*Thunder. First* Apparition, *an armed head, rises from*
*the cauldron.*

MACBETH: Tell me, thou unknown power—

FIRST WITCH:     He knows thy thought:
 Hear his speech, but say thou nought.   70

FIRST APPARITION: Macbeth! Macbeth! Macbeth! beware
 Macduff;
 Beware the Thane of Fife. Dismiss me. Enough. ①
          [*Descends.*

MACBETH: Whate'er thou art, for thy good caution thanks;
 Thou hast harped my fear aright. But one word more—

FIRST WITCH: He will not be commanded: here's another,
 More potent than the first.     76

*Thunder. Second* Apparition, *a bloody child, rises from*
*the cauldron.*

SECOND APPARITION: Macbeth! Macbeth! Macbeth!—

MACBETH: Had I three ears, I'd hear thee.

SECOND APPARITION: Be bloody, bold, and resolute: laugh to
 scorn
 The power of man, for none of woman born ② 80
 Shall harm Macbeth.     [*Descends.*

MACBETH: Then live, Macduff: what need I fear of thee?

84 *take a bond of*　bind by a legal bond.

85 so that I can prove my cowardly fears to be groundless.

86 *in spite of thunder*　even through thunder, such as now rumbles.

S.D.　The third apparition is the crowned child Malcolm, holding a tree like those he later orders his soldiers to hew and carry as camouflage.

87 *issue*　child.

88 *round And top*　crown and highest symbol.

91 *chafes*　rages.

92 Birnam and Dunsinane are twelve miles apart, near Perth.

94 *That will never be.*　Again, Macbeth does not consider the possibility of equivocation.

94-101 Macbeth speaks in rhyme, like the apparitions, sounding as certain of his future as they are.

95-6 *Who can . . . root?*　He asks the rhetorical question triumphantly.

95 *impress*　conscript.

96 *bodements*　prophecies.

97 *head*　armed force of the 'conspirers' in line 91.

98 *our high-placed Macbeth.*　The phrase rings with confidence: he sounds like the witches' masters.

99 *lease of nature*　natural span of life.

100 *mortal custom*　the natural course of death.

100-3 *Yet my . . . kingdom?*　After crowing with exultant relief, he now speaks in dread. The word 'Throbs' is highly vivid.

103 *this kingdom.*　The witches did not specify, in 1.3.67, where Banquo's descendants would reign. Macbeth hopes he has found a loophole in the prophecy. *Seek to . . . more.*　Their injunction exasperates him.

106 *noise*　music.

But yet I'll make assurance double sure,
And take a bond of fate: thou shalt not live,
That I may tell pale-hearted fear it lies, 85
And sleep in spite of thunder.

*Thunder. Third Apparition, a child crowned, with a tree*
*in his hand, rises from the cauldron.*

                What is this,
That rises like the issue of a king,
And wears upon his baby brow the round
And top of sovereignty?

ALL:             Listen, but speak not to't.

THIRD APPARITION: Be lion-mettled, proud, and take no care 90
Who chafes, who frets, or where conspirers are:
Macbeth shall never vanquished be until
Great Birnam wood to high Dunsinane hill
Shall come against him.           [*Descends.*

MACBETH:       That will never be:
Who can impress the forest, bid the tree 95
Unfix his earth-bound root? Sweet bodements! good!
Rebellion's head, rise never till the wood
Or Birnam rise, and our high-placed Macbeth
Shall live the lease of nature, pay his breath
To time and mortal custom. Yet my heart 100
Throbs to know one thing: tell me (if your art
Can tell so much) shall Banquo's issue ever
Reign in this kingdom?

ALL:             Seek to know no more.

MACBETH: I will be satisfied: deny me this,
And an eternal curse fall on you! Let me know. 105
          [*The cauldron descends. Oboes play.*
Why sinks that cauldron? and what noise is this?

FIRST WITCH: Show!

SECOND WITCH: Show!

THIRD WITCH: Show!

ALL:           Show his eyes, and grieve his heart; 110
           Come like shadows, so depart.

[ 115 ]

*S.D.* The procession consists of the eight Stuart kings, ancestors of James I. Do the kings simply cross the stage in single file, or do they form a group and mime with stately gestures? Macbeth's running commentary indicates some of the properties they carry.

Dumb-shows were a normal feature of Elizabethan and Jacobean drama.

116 *Start,* from your sockets, so that I can see no more.

117 *crack of doom* peal of the last trump.

119 *glass* magic mirror; or, crystal for showing the future.

120 *some,* kings of both England and Scotland. This is a tribute to James I, whose descendants would inherit the throne which he had united.

121 *two-fold balls* orbs used in two coronations, one at Scone and one at Westminster. *treble sceptres* one sceptre used in the Scottish coronation and two in the English.

123 *blood-boltered* with hair matted in blood.

124 Macbeth gazes at Banquo, and the apparitions vanish; he turns in amazement to the witches, and they have vanished too. Although they do not appear again, their influence continues.

125–32 The lines are not by Shakespeare; see the introduction to 3.5.

127 *sprites* spirits, as in 2.3.79.

130 *antic round* grotesque dance in a circle.

131–2 Perhaps this is a compliment to James I in the audience, as well as a reference to Macbeth.

132 *duties* respects.

135 Despite his antipathy to Macbeth, shown in 3.6, Lennox still serves him and has been on guard outside the cavern.

139 Macbeth trusts them, and he is damned.

*A show of Eight Kings, the last with a glass in his hand :*
BANQUO'S Ghost *following.*

MACBETH: Thou art too like the spirit of Banquo; down!
Thy crown does sear mine eyeballs. And thy hair,
Thou other gold-bound brow, is like the first.
A third is like the former. Filthy hags!                        *115*
Why do you show me this? A fourth? Start, eyes!
What, will the line stretch out to the crack of doom?
Another yet? A seventh? I'll see no more:
And yet the eighth appears, who bears a glass
Which shows me many more; and some I see             *120*
That two-fold balls and treble sceptres carry.
Horrible sight! Now I see 'tis true,
For the blood-bolter'd Banquo smiles upon me,
And points at them for his.              [*Apparitions vanish.*
                              What! is this so?
FIRST WITCH: Ay, sir, all this is so. But why             *125*
Stands Macbeth thus amazedly?
Come, sisters, cheer we up his sprites,
And show the best of our delights.
I'll charm the air to give a sound,
While you perform your antic round,                     *130*
That this great king may kindly say
Our duties did his welcome pay.
                    [*Music. The Witches dance, and vanish.*
MACBETH: Where are they? Gone? Let this pernicious hour
Stand aye accursed in the calendar!
Come in, without there!

*Enter* LENNOX.

LENNOX:                What's your Grace's will?       *135*
MACBETH: Saw you the Weird Sisters?
LENNOX:                            No, my lord.
MACBETH: Came they not by you?
LENNOX:                            No indeed, my lord.
MACBETH: Infected by the air whereon they ride,
And damned all those that trust them! I did hear
The galloping of horse: who was't came by?             *140*

In this drawing of a performance at Whitehall Palace, Macbeth
stares at the eighth king, who holds a convex mirror—a fashionable
novelty in 1606. It reflects James I in the front row of the audience.
The curtains are held apart by witches for the procession of kings,
and behind the opening stands the ghost of Banquo. In accordance
with stage convention of the time, his face is powdered white and
he wears a shiny, black cloak. A character so presented would be
immediately recognized as a ghost, in that age when the public
believed in ghosts as firmly as in witches.

The witches' garments are based on an illustration in Holinshed's
Chronicle, with the addition of symbolic, bat-like wings and decora-
tions that might have adorned theatrical costumes of the time. The
drawing on page 5 shows more clearly a fabric design of the evil
eye, and a skirt patterned with toads and insects, witches' familiars.
Symbolism was readily understood by an educated audience at a
royal command performance. When the King's Men were sum-
moned to act at court, their costumes looked particularly fine in the
glow of candlelight.

However, what mattered most in the performance was, as always,
the acting. If speech and movement are poor, even the most beauti-
ful costumes and subtlest lighting are wasted. Shakespeare's own
highly trained company spoke their lines and controlled their
gestures with fine skill. They were disciplined artists.

142 Macbeth hears this news for the first time: Lennox was told it in confidence at 3.6.29–39. His revelation now confirms Macbeth's belief in the apparitions.

144 *anticipat'st* forestallest.
145 *flighty* swift.

147–8 the very first conceptions of my heart shall be the first things I do. This is a highly significant moment: Macbeth finally forswears rational action, and makes his fate inevitable.

150 *surprise* seize.
At 3.4.139–40 Macbeth considered acting on impulse: why did he delay and visit the witches? Now, frantic at the show of kings, he determines not to hesitate again: did the second Apparition have any effect on his attitude to Macduff? What, in this scene, has made Macbeth feel more secure, and what has made him more desperate?

*Macduff's castle in Fife*

A chair for Lady Macduff can show that this is a domestic scene. Her son witnesses her acute distress and Ross's attempts as a comforter.

By keeping his wife innocent of his going to England, Macduff hoped to protect her from Macbeth's reprisals. She fears that cowardice has made him flee.

2 *patience* self-control.
3–4 *When our . . . traitors* when we are not really traitors, our actions make us seem to be.

7 *titles* possessions.
9 *wants the natural touch* lacks a father's natural protective instinct. *poor* feeble.
9, 11 *wren, owl.* The nesting wren is more directly symbolic than the martlet in 1.6.3–10. When, in this play, has the owl been mentioned, and what does it symbolize here?

12 *fear*, for himself. *love*, for his wife and children.

LENNOX: 'Tis two or three, my lord, that bring you word
  Macduff is fled to England.

MACBETH:                   Fled to England!

LENNOX: Ay, my good lord.

MACBETH. [*Aside.*] Time, thou anticipat'st my dread exploits;
  The flighty purpose never is o'ertook             *145*
  Unless the deed go with it. From this moment
  The very firstlings of my heart shall be
  The firstlings of my hand. And even now,
  To crown my thoughts with acts, be it thought and done:
  The castle of Macduff I will surprise,             *150*
  Seize upon Fife, give to the edge of the sword
  His wife, his babes, and all unfortunate souls
  That trace him in his line. No boasting like a fool:
  This deed I'll do before this purpose cool.
  But no more sights! [*Aloud.*] Where are these gentlemen? *155*
  Come, bring me where they are.            [*Exeunt.*

## SCENE TWO

*Enter* LADY MACDUFF, *her* Son, *and* ROSS.

LADY MACDUFF: What had he done to make him fly the land?

ROSS: You must have patience, madam.

LADY MACDUFF:                He had none;
  His flight was madness. When our actions do not,
  Our fears do make us traitors.

ROSS:              You know not
  Whether it was his wisdom or his fear.           5

LADY MACDUFF: Wisdom! to leave his wife, to leave his babes,
  His mansion and his titles, in a place
  From whence himself does fly? He loves us not;
  He wants the natural touch; for the poor wren,
  The most diminutive of birds, will fight—        *10*
  Her young ones in her nest—against the owl.
  All is the fear and nothing is the love;
  As little is the wisdom, where the flight
  So runs against all reason.

14 *coz* cousin, a general term indicating any close relationship.

15 *school* control. *for* as for.

16–17 *knows . . . season* understands the convulsions of the time.

18–19 *when . . . ourselves* when we are considered traitors without realising it.

19–20 *hold rumour from what we fear* accept rumours because we are afraid.

20 *yet know not what we fear* although our fears are vague.

21–2 *float . . . move* our storm-tossed feelings float and veer in all directions.

25 *cousin* Macduff's little son.

28–9 If Ross stayed, he would weep, and so cause embarrassment.

30 *Sirrah,* a word of address used by parents to children, as well as by masters to servants.

30 *dead,* as far as we're concerned, because we shall never see him again.

30–62 The mother's deep grief and her son's superficial brightness are in poignant contrast.

32 *birds.* He heard his mother talk about birds at lines 9–11, and perhaps he knows Matthew 6: 26: 'Behold the fowls of the air . . . your heavenly father feedeth them.' *with* on.

34 *lime* bird-lime, gluey stuff spread on twigs to catch birds. *pitfall* fowler's snare. *gin* trap.

36 *Poor birds . . . for* they are not set to catch wretched little birds like me. He puns on the adjective she has just used.

39–61 This is mostly in prose, which is suitable for questions and answers.

41 *to sell again,* because you will not want them all.

42–3 that remark taxes all your limited wisdom; and yet, indeed, you are quite intelligent enough for a child of your age.

44 *traitor.* The boy listened to 4–18.

ROSS:      My dearest coz,
 I pray you, school yourself: <u>but, for your husband,</u>  *15*
 <u>He is noble, wise, judicious, and best knows</u>
 <u>The fits o'the season.</u> I dare not speak much further:
 But cruel are the times, when we are traitors
 And do not know ourselves; when we hold rumour
 From what we fear, yet know not what we fear,  *20*
 But float upon a wild and violent sea
 Each way, and move—I take my leave of you:
 Shall not be long but I'll be here again.
 Things at the worst will cease, or else climb upward
 To what they were before. My pretty cousin,  *25*
 Blessing upon you!
LADY MACDUFF: Fathered he is, and yet he's fatherless.
ROSS: I am so much a fool, should I stay longer,
 It would be my disgrace and your discomfort:
 I take my leave at once.    [*Exit.*
LADY MACDUFF:    Sirrah, your father's dead:  *30*
 And what will you do now? How will you live?
SON: As birds do, mother.
LADY MACDUFF:    What, with worms and flies?
SON: With what I get, I mean; and so do they.
LADY MACDUFF: Poor Bird! thou'dst never fear the net
  nor lime,
 The pitfall nor the gin.  *35*
SON: Why should I, mother? Poor birds they are not
  set for.
 My father is not dead, for all your saying.
LADY MACDUFF: Yes, he is dead: how wilt thou do for a
 father?
SON: Nay, how will you do for a husband?
LADY MACDUFF: Why, I can buy me twenty at any market.  *40*
SON: Then you'll buy 'em to sell again.
LADY MACDUFF: Thou speak'st with all thy wit; and yet,
  i' faith,
 With wit enough for thee.
SON: Was my father a traitor, mother?

[ 123 ]

45 *he was,* in abandoning his family and turning against his king and country.

47 *swears and lies* breaks his oath of allegiance to his king; or, breaks his marriage-vow. The porter admitted an equivocator to hell at 2.3.8–11. This may be another reference to Father Garnet.

54-6 The boy's tenacious questions lead to his triumphant conclusion; but in his innocence, he is unaware of the power of evil.
55 *enow* enough.

57 *monkey* clever little fellow. Depite her grief, she is amused by his sharpness. The next line, a repetition of 38, she speaks seriously.
1-62 How has Shakespeare built up sympathy for Lady Macduff? What is the dramatic purpose of this episode of natural affection?

62 Perhaps she draws the boy to her.

63-71 How does this speech increase the dramatic excitement?
64 although I am perfectly aware that you are an honoured lady.
65 *doubt* fear.
66 *homely* lowly.

68 *To ... thus* in alarming you with this warning.
69 *To do worse to you* not to warn you; also, to harm you.
70 *Which is ... person* and fell cruelty is too close to you.

74 *sometime* sometimes.

LADY MACDUFF: Ay, that he was. 45

SON: What is a traitor?

LADY MACDUFF: Why, one that swears and lies.

SON: And be all traitors that do so?

LADY MACDUFF: Every one that does so is a traitor, and must be hanged.

SON: And must they all be hanged that swear and lie? 50

LADY MACDUFF: Every one.

SON: Who must hang them?

LADY MACDUFF: Why, the honest men.

SON: Then the liars and swearers are fools; for there are liars and swearers enow to beat the honest men and hang up 55 them.

LADY MACDUFF: Now God help thee, poor monkey! But how wilt thou do for a father?

SON: If he were dead, you'd weep for him: if you would not, it were a good sign that I should quickly have a new 60 father.

LADY MACDUFF: Poor prattler, how thou talk'st!

*Enter a* Messenger.

MESSENGER: Bless you, fair dame! I am not to you known, Though in your state of honour I am perfect. I doubt some danger does approach you nearly. 65 If you will take a homely man's advice, Be not found here; hence, with your little ones. To fright you thus, methinks, I am too savage; To do worse to you were fell cruelty, Which is too nigh your person. Heaven preserve you! 70 I dare abide no longer.                 [*Exit.*

LADY MACDUFF:          Whither should I fly? I have done no harm. But I remember now I am in this earthly world, where to do harm Is often laudable, to do good sometime Accounted dangerous folly: why then, alas! 75 Do I put up that womanly defence, To say I have done no harm?

79–80 *I hope . . . him.* The murderers, sent by fiendish Macbeth, look suited to their devilish task of destroying sanctified family life. Macduff's flight has been associated with piety by 3.6.26–31, 45–9.

81 *Thou liest.* The boy has intuitively perceived the truth about his father, and now springs loyally to his defence, attacking the murderer with his fists or with a knife. *shag-haired* shaggy-haired. *egg* unhatched weakling.

82 *Young fry* spawn.

Compare Lady Macduff with Lady Macbeth.

*Macbeth* is a gory play. Shakespeare's audience, delighting in dramatic violence and bloodshed, expected murder to look real. It is arguable that modern dress, as shown in the drawing opposite, adds impact to the wanton cruelty of this killing.

*Enter* Murderers.

                       What are these faces?

MURDERER: Where is your husband?

LADY MACDUFF: I hope in no place so unsanctified
  Where such as thou mayst find him.

MURDERER:                He's a traitor.     *80*

SON: Thou liest, thou shag-haired villain.

MURDERER:           What, you egg! [*Stabbing him.*
  Young fry of treachery!

SON:              He has killed me, mother:
  Run away, I pray you!             [*Dies.*
       [*Exeunt* LADY MACDUFF, *crying 'Murder!'*

*Outside the palace of Edward the Confessor, in England*

The change of country can be shown by fresh emblems on banners, curtains or scenery. A suitable symbol of the piety of England would be the cross; and plainsong or other religious music might introduce the scene.

Malcolm, who fears that Macduff may be yet another of Macbeth's spies sent to lure the rightful king of Scotland into the tyrant's clutches, tests Macduff's loyalty. Anyone who escapes through the iron curtain surrounding the police state, and tries to make Malcolm return, is naturally suspect. We last saw Malcolm in 2.3.

1–8 Malcolm implies that he is prepared to do nothing but weep: Macduff tries to make him return to Scotland and fight.

3 *mortal* deadly.

4 *bestride* defend, like a warrior protecting a fallen comrade.
*birthdom* native land.

6 *that* so that. *it* heaven. The cries of Lady Macduff are still fresh in the audience's ears.

7 *felt* suffered.

8–17 Malcolm, in this speech, 8–11, refuses to act yet; 11–14, shows why Macduff may still be loyal to Macbeth; 14–17, suggests that Macduff may be willing to sacrifice Malcolm for gain.

8 *Like syllable of dolour* the same cry of grief. *I believe* I am sure has happened. *wail* lament.

10 *As* when. *to friend* favourable.

12 *sole* mere.

13 *loved him well* served him very loyally.

14 *He hath . . . yet.* News of the murders at Fife has not yet reached Macduff or Malcolm. *young*, and therefore not dangerous.

14–15 *something you . . . me* you may earn a reward from him for deceiving me.

15 *and wisdom* and it might be wise.

18 Macduff speaks with great indignation.

20 *imperial* royal.

19–20 *may recoil . . . charge* is likely to give way under pressure from a king. *recoil*, like a gun or a line of troops.

20 *But I . . . pardon* Malcolm apologizes for hurting Macduff's feelings, but continues to test his loyalty in the knowledge that real goodness is incorruptible.

21 *transpose* change.

## SCENE THREE

*Enter* MALCOLM *and* MACDUFF

MALCOLM: Let us seek out some desolate shade, and there
  Weep our sad bosoms empty.

MACDUFF:                Let us rather
  Hold fast the mortal sword, and like good men
  Bestride our down-fall'n birthdom. Each new morn
  New widows howl, new orphans cry; new sorrows      *5*
  Strike heaven on the face, that it resounds
  As if it felt with Scotland and yelled out
  Like syllable of dolour.

MALCOLM:             What I believe, I'll wail;
  What know, believe; and what I can redress,
  As I shall find the time to friend, I will.      *10*
  What you have spoke, it may be so perchance.
  This tyrant, whose sole name blisters our tongues,
  Was once thought honest; you have loved him well;
  He hath not touched you yet. I am young; but something
  You may deserve of him through me; and wisdom      *15*
  To offer up a weak, poor, innocent lamb
  To appease an angry god.

MACDUFF: I am not treacherous.

MALCOLM:              But Macbeth is.
  A good and virtuous nature may recoil
  In an imperial charge. But I shall crave your pardon;      *20*
  That which you are, my thoughts cannot transpose;

**22** there are still good angels, although the brightest angel of all, Lucifer, fell from heaven. The analogy is a reminder of Macbeth, the radiant general who committed sacrilege.

**23** *would* might try to.

**23-4** even if all evil things wore the shining countenance of goodness, yet goodness would still have a shining countenance too. Duncan knew that 'There's no art to find the mind's construction in the face' (1.4.11-12), but nevertheless he allowed himself to be fatally deceived: his son is determined not to make the same mistake, but he wants to soothe Macduff's wounded feelings.

**24** *I have ... hopes,* because Malcolm mistrusts me.

**25** *there where ... doubts* by that hasty action of yours which has made me suspicious.

**26** *rawness* unprotected state.

**26-8** Malcolm thinks that Macduff must have guarded his family by an agreement with the unscrupulous Macbeth. In Malcolm's position, would you have thought so too?

**29-30** *Let not ... safeties* do not let my suspicions dishonour you: they are my self-protection. *rightly just* perfectly honourable.

**31-3** Macduff turns away in despair.

**33** *goodness* Malcolm's goodness. *wear thou thy wrongs* flaunt your crimes.

**34** *The title* the tyrant's title to the throne. *affeered* legally confirmed. There is a serious pun on 'afeared'.

**37** *to boot* in addition.

**38** *absolute* certain.

**42** *in* to support.

**43** *England* King of England.

**44-114** Malcolm now pretends that he is a most vicious man, and potentially a worse king than Macbeth. He heaps sins on himself to see whether Macduff nonetheless wants him to return to Scotland. If Macduff does want an even worse king, then his attempt to lure Malcolm back to Scotland cannot be purposed for the country's good.

**47** *have* endure.

**49** *What should he be?* who can you be talking about?

**51** *grafted* made part of myself, like a graft in a tree.

**52** *opened,* like buds.

**54** *as a lamb.* At line 16 Malcolm was the lamb.

**55** *confineless harms* limitless evils.

Angels are bright still, though the brightest fell.
Though all things foul would wear the brows of grace,
Yet grace must still look so.

MACDUFF:                         I have lost my hopes.

MALCOLM: Perchance even there where I did find my doubts.   25
  Why in that rawness left you wife and child—
  Those precious motives, those strong knots of love—
  Without leave-taking? I pray you,
  Let not my jealousies be your dishonours,
  But mine own safeties: you may be rightly just,   30
  Whatever I shall think.

MACDUFF:                         Bleed, bleed, poor country!
  Great tyranny, lay thou thy basis sure,
  For goodness dare not check thee: wear thou thy wrongs,
  The title is affeered! Fare thee well, lord:
  I would not be the villain that thou think'st   35
  For the whole space that's in the tyrant's grasp,
  And the rich East to boot.

MALCOLM:                         Be not offended:
  I speak not as in absolute fear of you.
  I think our country sinks beneath the yoke;
  It weeps, it bleeds, and each new day a gash   40
  Is added to her wounds. I think withal
  There would be hands uplifted in my right;
  And here from gracious England have I offer
  Of goodly thousands. But, for all this,
  When I shall tread upon the tyrant's head,   45
  Or wear it on my sword, yet my poor country
  Shall have more vices than it had before,
  More suffer, and more sundry ways than ever,
  By him that shall succeed.

MACDUFF:                         What should he be?

MALCOLM: It is myself I mean; in whom I know   50
  All the particulars of vice so grafted
  That, when they shall be opened, black Macbeth
  Will seem as pure as snow, and the poor state
  Esteem him as a lamb, being compared
  With my confineless harms.

57 *top* surpass.

57–100 Through Malcolm's list of royal sins, Shakespeare indicates what its opposite must be: the virtues of an ideal king are implied. The episode would have delighted James I, who was fascinated by the theory of kingship.

58 *Luxurious* lustful. Macbeth is neither lustful nor avaricious: but Malcolm is comparing himself to the most vicious king he can imagine—an even more sinful Macbeth, particularly prone to Malcolm's pretended vices. In Holinshed's *Chronicle* Malcolm accuses himself of lust, avarice and deceit.

59 *Sudden* violent.

61 *voluptuousness* lust.

61–2 *your* Scotland's.

64 *continent* restraining; also, chaste.

65 *will* lust.

67 *In nature . . . tyranny* is a tyranny over the kingdom of a man's nature. Shakespeare frequently shows that order is essential to harmonious living: the peace of the universe, of the realm and of the individual all depend on order.

69 *yet* despite all that you have said.

71 *Convey* secretly conduct. *spacious* lavish.

72 *seem cold* appear chaste. *time* world, as in 1.7.81.

75 as will sacrifice their virtue to a king.

76 *it* him, the vulture that represents Malcolm's ravenous appetite.

77 *ill-composed* unbalanced. *affection* temperament.

78 *stanchless* insatiable.

79 *cut off* kill.

80 *his* that man's.

85 *sticks*, like a sword, and like a root.

86 *summer-seeming* like summer in its heat and brevity.

86–7 *been the sword . . . kings* caused the death of those Scottish kings who have been murdered.

88 *foisons* abundant supplies.

MACDUFF:                                      Not in the legions          **55**
    Of horrid hell can come a devil more damned
    In evils to top Macbeth.
MALCOLM:                            I grant him bloody,
    Luxurious, avaricious, false, deceitful,
    Sudden, malicious, smacking of every sin
    That has a name: but there's no bottom, none,          **60**
    In my voluptuousness. Your wives, your daughters,
    Your matrons and your maids, could not fill up
    The cistern of my lust, and my desire
    All continent impediments would o'erbear
    That did oppose my will. Better Macbeth          **65**
    Than such an one to reign.
MACDUFF:                            Boundless intemperance
    In nature is a tyranny; it hath been
    Th'untimely emptying of the happy throne
    And fall of many kings. But fear not yet
    To take upon you what is yours: you may          **70**
    Convey your pleasures in a spacious plenty,
    And yet seem cold, the time you may so hoodwink.
    We have willing dames enough; there cannot be
    That vulture in you, to devour so many
    As will to greatness dedicate themselves,          **75**
    Finding it so inclined.
MALCOLM:                      With this there grows
    In my most ill-composed affection such
    A stanchless avarice that, were I king,
    I should cut off the nobles for their lands,
    Desire his jewels and this other's house;          **80**
    And my more-having would be as a sauce
    To make me hunger more, that I should forge
    Quarrels unjust against the good and loyal,
    Destroying them for wealth.
MACDUFF:                            This avarice
    Sticks deeper, grows with more pernicious root          **85**
    Than summer-seeming lust; and it hath been
    The sword of our slain kings: yet do not fear;
    Scotland hath foisons to fill up your will,

**89** *Of your mere own* entirely yours, because they are royal property. *portable* bearable.

**90** counterbalanced by your other qualities.

**91-4** James I wrote *Basilikon Doron*, precepts for his son on the art of government, and in it he listed 'justice . . . clemency, magnanimity, liberality, constancy, humility, and all other princely virtues'.

**94** *fortitude* constancy.

**95** *relish* trace.

**96** *the division of* variations on; the metaphor is from music. *each several* every sort of.

**98** As Lady Macbeth had, in a way, done at 1.5.46-9. Compare also 1.5.16. *concord* harmony.

**99** *Uproar* throw into confusion. *confound* disrupt, as Macbeth was willing for the witches to do on his behalf at 4.1.52-60

**104** *untitled* usurping.

**106** since the truest heir, Malcolm.

**107** *interdiction* self-accusation.

**108** *blaspheme his breed* slander his parentage.

**111** *Died every . . . lived* lived each day as holily as if it were her last. St. Paul declared, in 1 Corinthians 15: 31, 'I die daily'.

**111-14** Macduff's horrified misery proves that he is not an agent of Macbeth, and Malcolm is satisfied that Macduff has passed the test.

**112** *repeat* recite. *upon* against, as at line 131.

**113** *banished*, because Macbeth's evils are those now claimed by Malcolm.

**114-37** Malcolm, in this speech, 114-17, says that he is reassured; 117-20, shows that experience has taught him to be careful; 120-31, swears that he has been lying about himself; 131-2, declares his willingness to fight; 133-7, reveals that plans are already afoot and that he is ready to go.

**116** *black scruples* dark suspicions.

**118** *trains* plots.

**119** *modest* restraining.

**120-1** *but God . . . me.* Malcolm, swearing a solemn oath, raises his right hand.

**123** *Unspeak* deny. *mine own detraction* my slanders of myself. *abjure* renounce.

Of your mere own. All these are portable,
With other graces weighed.                                    *90*

MALCOLM: But I have none. The king-becoming graces,
As justice, verity, temperance, stableness,
Bounty, perseverance, mercy, lowliness,
Devotion, patience, courage, fortitude,
I have no relish of them, but abound                          *95*
In the division of each several crime,
Acting it many ways. Nay, had I power, I should
Pour the sweet milk of concord into hell,
Uproar the universal peace, confound
All unity on earth.

MACDUFF:                     O Scotland, Scotland!          *100*

MALCOLM: If such a one be fit to govern, speak:
I am as I have spoken.

MACDUFF:                     <u>Fit to govern!</u>
<u>No, not to live.</u> O nation miserable,
With an untitled tyrant bloody-sceptred,
When shalt thou see thy wholesome days again,                *105*
Since that the truest issue of thy throne
By his own interdiction stands accursed,
And does blaspheme his breed? Thy royal father
Was a most sainted king; the queen that bore thee,
Oft'ner upon her knees than on her feet,                     *110*
Died every day she lived. Fare thee well!
These evils thou repeat'st upon thyself
Hath banished me from Scotland. O my breast,
Thy hope ends here!

MALCOLM:                     Macduff, this noble passion,
Child of integrity, hath from my soul                        *115*
Wiped the black scruples, reconciled my thoughts
To thy good truth and honour. Devilish Macbeth
By many of these trains hath sought to win me
Into his power, and modest wisdom plucks me
From over-credulous haste: <u>but God above</u>               *120*
Deal between thee and me! for even now
I put myself to thy direction, and
Unspeak mine own detraction, here abjure

125 *For* as being.

126 *Unknown to woman* virgin. *was forsworn* perjured myself.

127 *coveted* desired.

134 *Old Siward.* See 3.6.31.

135 *at a point* prepared for action.

136–7 *the chance . . . quarrel* may our chance of success be as certain as the justice of our cause.

137 *Why are you silent?* Macduff is now speechless with surprise and relief. Has Malcolm handled the situation in an inexperienced, tactless way, or was his approach unavoidable? Has the scene so far been dramatically effective?

140–59 The supernatural, healing powers of a saintly king are described in this static interlude: they expose, by contrast, the murderous violence of a tyrant who relies on black magic.

140 *the King*, Edward the Confessor. James I was descended from him.

142 *stay* await. *his cure.* Edward the Confessor had the miraculous power of curing scrofula, a disease in which the glands swell and break out through the skin. His successors to the throne inherited the power. James I kept up the ceremony of touching the sufferers, although he thought that any subsequent relief came from the patient's faith rather than from miracle. *convinces* defeats.

143 *assay of art* efforts of medical science.

145 *presently* instantly.

146 *the evil*, and 'the king's evil', are other names for scrofula.

149 *solicits heaven* induces heaven's aid.

150 *strangely visited* extraordinarily afflicted.

The taints and blames I laid upon myself
For strangers to my nature. I am yet                              *125*
Unknown to woman, never was forsworn,
Scarcely have coveted what was mine own,
At no time broke my faith, would not betray
The devil to his fellow, and delight
No less in truth than life: my first false speaking    *130*
Was this upon myself. What I am truly
Is thine and my poor country's to command:
Whither indeed, before thy here-approach,
Old Siward, with ten thousand war-like men
Already at a point, was setting forth.                          *135*
Now we'll together, and the chance of goodness
Be like our warranted quarrel! Why are you silent?
MACDUFF: Such welcome and unwelcome things at once
  'Tis hard to reconcile.

*Enter an English* Doctor.

MALCOLM: Well, more anon. Comes the King forth, I pray
  you?                                                                    *140*
DOCTOR: Ay, sir; there are a crew of wretched souls
  That stay his cure. Their malady convinces
  The great assay of art; but at his touch,
  Such sanctity hath heaven given his hand,
  They presently amend.
MALCOLM:                       I thank you, doctor.              *145*
                                           [*Exit* Doctor.
MACDUFF: What's the disease he means?
MALCOLM:                                        'Tis called the evil:
  A most miraculous work in this good king,
  Which often, since my here-remain in England,
  I have seen him do. How he solicits heaven,
  Himself best knows; but strangely-visited people,   *150*
  All swoln and ulcerous, pitiful to the eye,

The drawing of the English doctor on page 136 is based on a portrait of Sir Theodore Mayerne, James I's physician, who may conceivably have played the part at a special Court performance. Many old men wore skull caps and carried walking-sticks.

152 *mere*  utter.
153 *stamp*  stamped gold coin, called an 'angel'.
154 *spoken*  said.

156 *healing benediction*  blessed gift of healing.
157 James I's bishops said that he also had this.

159 Ross enters very slowly: his face is probably muffled.
160 Malcolm recognises Ross's costume as Scottish. He diplomatically prefers not to know the man, who may be a spy from Macbeth: but Macduff's greeting reassures Malcolm. Ross's chief dramatic function is to deliver news: does Shakespeare give him character or treat him, here and elsewhere, only as a mouthpiece?
161 Perhaps Ross kneels in homage to Malcolm.
163 *means*  obstacles, such as Macbeth's reign and his attempts to entrap Malcolm.

166 *nothing*  no-one.

170 *A modern ecstasy*  a trivial excitement.
170-1 *the dead man's . . . who*  people scarcely bother to ask for whom the bell tolls.

173 *or ere they sicken*  before the flowers wither; or, before the good men are taken ill (because they are suddenly slaughtered).
173-4 *relation too nice*  narration too elaborate.

175 news only an hour old makes the speaker's audience hiss, because the agonies of the past hour have made that news stale.
176 *teems*  spawns.
177-9 *well . . . well . . . well at peace.*  Ross deliberately puns: he cannot yet summon enough courage to declare the news from Fife. Peace, death and health were linked by Macbeth in 3.2.20-3.

The mere despair of surgery, he cures,
Hanging a golden stamp about their necks,
Put on with holy prayers; and 'tis spoken,
To the succeeding royalty he leaves                    155
The healing benediction. With this strange virtue
He hath a heavenly gift of prophecy,
And sundry blessings hang about his throne
That speak him full of grace.

*Enter* ROSS.

MACDUFF:                              See, who comes here?
MALCOLM: My countryman; but yet I know him not.        160
MACDUFF: My ever-gentle cousin, welcome hither.
MALCOLM: I know him now. Good God, betimes remove
  The means that makes us strangers!
ROSS:                              Sir, amen.
MACDUFF: Stands Scotland where it did?
ROSS:                              Alas, poor country,
  Almost afraid to know itself! It cannot              165
  Be called our mother, but our grave; where nothing,
  But who knows nothing, is once seen to smile;
  Where sighs and groans and shrieks that rend the air
  Are made, not marked; where violent sorrows seems
  A modern ecstasy; the dead man's knell               170
  Is there scarce asked for who; and good men's lives
  Expire before the flowers in their caps,
  Dying or ere they sicken.
MACDUFF.                    O, relation
  Too nice, and yet too true!
MALCOLM:                    What's the newest grief?
ROSS: That of an hour's age doth hiss the speaker;     175
  Each minute teems a new one.
MACDUFF:                    How does my wife?
ROSS: Why, well.
MACDUFF:        And all my children?
ROSS:                              Well too.
MACDUFF: The tyrant has not battered at their peace?

180 *niggard*  miser.

181 Ross ignores Macduff's question and turns to Malcolm.

183 *out*  had left home to fight against Macbeth.

184 which was confirmed in my belief.

185 *For that*  because. *power afoot*  army mobilizing.

186 *of*  for.

187 *make our*  make even our.

188 *doff*  throw off, like clothes. Alliteration makes the line
emphatic.

189 *England*  King of England, as in line 43.

192 *gives out*  proclaims. *Would*  I wish I could.

194 *would*  should.

195 *should not latch*  could not catch.

196 *The general cause*  public matters. *fee-grief*  grief that has a
particular owner.

202 *possess*  inform.

203 *Humh!*  Not a word, but a heartbroken groan.

204–7 When he hears the news, Macduff hides his face.

205–6 *To relate the manner, Were*  to describe the way they were
killed, would be.

206 *quarry*  heap of slaughtered deer. *deer.*  This pun on 'dear'
is loaded with emotion.

ROSS: No; they were well at peace when I did leave 'em.

MACDUFF: Be not a niggard of your speech: how goes't?    *180*

ROSS: When I came hither to transport the tidings
    Which I have heavily borne, there ran a rumour
    <u>Of many worthy fellows that were out;</u>
    Which was to my belief witnessed the rather
    For that I saw the tyrant's power afoot.    *185*
    Now is the time of help; your eye in Scotland
    Would create soldiers, make our women fight,
    To doff their dire distresses.

MALCOLM:                     Be't their comfort
    We are coming thither. Gracious England hath
    Lent us good Siward and ten thousand men;    *190*
    An older and a better soldier none
    That Christendom gives out.

ROSS:                   Would I could answer
    This comfort with the like! But I have words
    That would be howled out in the desert air,
    Where hearing should not latch them.

MACDUFF:                 What concern they? *195*
    The general cause? or is it a fee-grief
    Due to some single breast?

ROSS:              No mind that's honest
    But in it shares some woe, though the main part
    Pertains to you alone.

MACDUFF:           If it be mine,
    Keep it not from me, quickly let me have it.    *200*

ROSS: Let not your ears despise my tongue for ever,
    Which shall possess them with the heaviest sound
    That ever yet they heard.

MACDUFF:           Humh! I guess at it.

ROSS: Your castle is surprised; your wife and babes
    Savagely slaughtered. To relate the manner,    *205*
    Were, on the quarry of these murdered deer,
    To add the death of you.

MALCOLM:          Merciful heaven!
    What, man! Ne'er pull your hat upon your brows;

210 *whispers* whispers to. *o'erfraught* overladen.

212 *must be* had to be.

216 *He* Macbeth, because his childlessness frustrates revenge or because a father could never have ordered the death of children; or perhaps Macduff refers to Malcolm, a brash youth who thinks he can arouse a bereaved man by thoughts of revenge at such a moment.

217 *hell-kite* hellish bird of prey, imagined as raiding a roost.

218 *dam* mother.

219 *fell* cruel. *Dispute* fight against.

222 *heaven.* The messenger's prayer at 4.2.70 has not been granted.

224 *Naught* evil.

225–6 *Not for . . . souls* not for their own sins, but for mine, slaughter fell on their souls. Macduff does not call leaving Scotland a sin: he had to be 'from thence' for the sake of his country: but he sees disaster as retribution for sin, and because the victims were innocent he blames himself.

226 *Heaven . . . now!* He crosses himself.

228 *Convert* change.

230 *front to front* face to face.

230–4 Perhaps Macduff clasps his hands in prayer.

231 *intermission* delay.

233–4 *if he 'scape . . . too* if I don't kill him, may God have mercy on his soul.

234 *This tune goes manly* this is a manly way to speak.

235 *power* army.

236 *Our . . . but* we need only. *our leave* King Edward's permission to go; also, to say our farewells.

237 *ripe,* like a fruit-tree. *powers,* angels of the order referred to at 2.1.7.

238 *Put on their instruments* arm themselves. *cheer* comfort. What has this scene added to the characters of Malcolm and Macduff? How has the holy background influenced our feelings about them and about Macbeth? Compare conditions in the English court with those in the Scottish court.

Give sorrow words. The grief that does not speak
Whispers the o'erfraught heart and bids it break.                    210

MACDUFF: My children too?

ROSS:                              Wife, children, servants, all
That could be found.

MACDUFF:                          And I must be from thence!
My wife killed too?

ROSS:                          I have said.

MALCOLM:                              Be comforted:
Let's make us medicines of our great revenge
To cure this deadly grief.                                          215

MACDUFF: He has no children. All my pretty ones?
Did you say all? O hell-kite! All?
What, all my pretty chickens and their dam
At one fell swoop?

MALCOLM:                          Dispute it like a man.

MACDUFF:                                      I shall do so;
But I must also feel it as a man:                                   220
I cannot but remember such things were
That were most precious to me. Did heaven look on,
And would not take their part? Sinful Macduff,
They were all struck for thee! Naught that I am,
Not for their own demerits, but for mine,                           225
Fell slaughter on their souls. Heaven rest them now!

MALCOLM: Be this the whetstone of your sword: let grief
Convert to anger; blunt not the heart, enrage it.

MACDUFF: O, I could play the woman with mine eyes
And braggart with my tongue. But, gentle heavens,                   230
Cut short all intermission; front to front
Bring thou this fiend of Scotland and myself;
Within my sword's length set him; if he 'scape,
Heaven forgive him too!

MALCOLM:                          This tune goes manly.
Come, go we to the King, our power is ready,                        235
Our lack is nothing but our leave. Macbeth
Is ripe for shaking, and the powers above
Put on their instruments. Receive what cheer you may;
The night is long that never finds the day.         [*Exeunt.*

[ 143 ]

# Macbeth

## In Macbeth's castle at Dunsinane

The doctor and lady-in-waiting speak in grave, hushed tones. After the heightened, emotional verse at the end of the previous scene, Shakespeare uses unadorned prose to create expectation and excitement.

4 *field* battlefield, to subdue the Scottish rebels. See 4.3.183.

5 *nightgown* dressing-gown, as at 2.2.71.

6 *closet* cabinet for papers. She may have been writing a letter to Macbeth, or a confession.

9–13 His speech is rather pompous and professional.

9 *perturbation* disturbance.

10 *effects of watching* deeds of waking.

11–12 *actual performances* acts.

14 *I will not.* Because Lady Macbeth's words were incriminating.

15 *meet* proper; he would treat her report with professional secrecy.

18 *This is her very guise* she is precisely as she was before. Shakespeare's contemporaries would have ascribed her sleep-walking to possession by demons: what do you ascribe it to?

19 *close* concealed: the lady-in-waiting and doctor move aside.

21–2 In her state of nervous collapse, Lady Macbeth cannot bear the dark; ironically, she invoked darkness at 1.5.49–53.

23–4 Lady Macbeth puts down the candle.

24 *sense* powers of sight.

# ACT FIVE

## SCENE ONE

*Enter a Scottish* Doctor *and a* Lady-in-Waiting.

DOCTOR: I have two nights watched with you, but can perceive no truth in your report. When was it she last walked?

LADY-IN-WAITING: Since his Majesty went into the field, I have seen her rise from her bed, throw her nightgown upon her, unlock her closet, take forth paper, fold it, write upon it, read it, afterwards seal it, and again return to bed; yet all this while in a most fast sleep. 5

DOCTOR: A great perturbation in nature, to receive at once the benefit of sleep and do the effects of watching! In this slumbery agitation, besides her walking and other actual performances, what, at any time, have you heard her say? 10

LADY-IN-WAITING: That, sir, which I will not report after her.

DOCTOR: You may to me, and 'tis most meet you should. 15

LADY-IN-WAITING: Neither to you nor any one, having no witness to confirm my speech.

*Enter* LADY MACBETH, *with a candle.*

Lo you, here she comes! This is her very guise; and, upon my life, fast asleep. Observe her, stand close.

DOCTOR: How came she by that light? 20

LADY-IN-WAITING: Why, it stood by her: she has light by her continually, 'tis her command.

DOCTOR: You see her eyes are open.

LADY-IN-WAITING: Ay, but their sense are shut.

DOCTOR: What is it she does now? Look how she rubs her hands. 25

LADY-IN-WAITING: It is an accustomed action with her, to seem thus washing her hands: I have known her to continue in this a quarter of an hour.

There were no actresses on the public stage in England before 1660. Female parts were played by boys, and this drawing shows a boy, aged about 15, as Lady Macbeth at the Globe Theatre. He wears a wig.

Boys were apprenticed to theatrical companies and learned their craft from busy actors. We know very little about the boys for whom Shakespeare wrote: Lady Macbeth's reference to her 'little' hand in line 49 may indicate that the original actor was light in build.

When a boy-player's voice broke, he could graduate to minor male parts and eventually to major ones. Membership of the King's Men was lucrative for those who, like Shakespeare, became directors. He made enough money to buy a fine house in Stratford-upon-Avon, and to spend most of his time there after reaching the age of 47. All his income came from his work for the King's Men and from investments. His colleagues, who collected and published his plays after his death, admired Shakespeare not only as a delightful, upright and gentle person, but also as a very shrewd man of the theatre.

30 *Yet* even now, after all this washing. *spot* stain. How has she been proved wrong since 2.2.68?

30–65 Lady Macbeth's broken prose is haunted by echoes of past events and past speeches.

31–2 The doctor decides to make notes. *satisfy* confirm.

33 *One, two;* the strokes of the bell she rang as a signal: see 2.1.31–2, 62.

34 *Hell is murky.* She is now in the hell which she wanted to surround her at 1.5.50.

35 *afeard;* she is haunted by her sarcasm at 1.7.39–41, 49.

36 *when none . . . account;* her despair echoes her bravado at 1.7.77–9.

37–8 *Yet who . . . him;* she remembers her surprise when she returned to Duncan's chamber at 2.2.58.

39 Why does he make this remark now?

40 *The Thane of Fife . . . wife.* What is the effect of this jingle about Lady Macduff?

42–3 *you mar . . . starting;* Macbeth's lack of self-control when he saw Banquo's ghost alarms her still, as it did at 3.4.61–6.

44 *Go to* yes, indeed.

44–5 Shocked by his patient's revelation, the doctor speaks his thoughts to her.

49–50 *Oh! oh! oh!* This probably represents one very long, profound sigh.

LADY MACBETH: Yet here's a spot. 30

DOCTOR: Hark, she speaks! I will set down what comes from
her, to satisfy my remembrance the more strongly.

LADY MACBETH: Out, damned spot! out, I say! One, two:
why, then 'tis time to do't. Hell is murky. Fie, my lord,
fie! a soldier, and afeard? What need we fear who knows 35
it, when none can call our power to account? Yet who
would have thought the old man to have had so much
blood in him?

DOCTOR: Do you mark that?

LADY MACBETH: The Thane of Fife had a wife: where is she 40
now? What, will these hands ne'er be clean? No more o'
that, my lord, no more o' that: you mar all with this
starting.

DOCTOR: Go to, go to: you have known what you should
not. 45

LADY-IN-WAITING: She has spoke what she should not, I am
sure of that: Heaven knows what she has known.

LADY MACBETH: Here's the smell of the blood still: all the
perfumes of Arabia will not sweeten this little hand. Oh!
oh! oh! 50

*a little*
*water*
*clears*
*us*
*of*
*this*
*deed*

[ 147 ]

51 *sorely charged*  painfully burdened.

53 *dignity*  worth.
54–5 The perplexed doctor wags his head, and the lady-in-waiting gives point to his vague use of *well*.

56 *practice*  medical skill.

61 *on's*  of his.
62 He is astonished by this further revelation.

64–5 *What's done . . . undone*  She repeats the cold comfort she gave at 3.2.12.

68 *Foul . . . abroad*  rumours of evil are widespread.
68–76 Verse closes the scene in formal orderliness.
69 *infected*  corrupted.
71 *the divine . . . physician*  a priest for her soul than a doctor for her body.
73 *means of all annoyance*  all means of harming herself. He fears that Lady Macbeth may commit suicide.
75 *mated*  stupefied.

What gives this scene its power?

### The country near Dunsinane

The 'worthy fellows' of 4.3.183, have deserted Macbeth and are on the march to join Malcolm and the English invaders. Drumming adds vigour to their brisk and businesslike entry.

1 *power*  army.
2 *uncle.*  Siward was, according to Holinshed, Malcolm's grandfather and Duncan's father-in-law. Shakespeare has increased Duncan's historical age, and to be consistent he makes Siward an uncle of Malcolm.
3 *dear causes*  grievous causes for revenge.
4 *alarm*  call to arms.

DOCTOR: What a sigh is there! The heart is sorely charged.

LADY-IN-WAITING: I would not have such a heart in my bosom
   for the dignity of the whole body.

DOCTOR: Well, well, well.

LADY-IN-WAITING: Pray God it be, sir.                          55

DOCTOR: This disease is beyond my practice: yet I have
   known those which have walked in their sleep who have
   died holily in their beds.

LADY MACBETH: Wash your hands, put on your nightgown,
   look not so pale: I tell you yet again, Banquo's buried; he  60
   cannot come out on's grave.

DOCTOR: Even so?

LADY MACBETH: To bed, to bed: there's knocking at the gate:
   come, come, come, come, give me your hand. What's done
   cannot be undone. To bed, to bed, to bed.        [*Exit.*  65

DOCTOR: Will she go now to bed?

LADY-IN-WAITING: Directly.

DOCTOR: Foul whisperings are abroad. Unnatural deeds
   Do breed unnatural troubles; infected minds
   To their deaf pillows will discharge their secrets.          70
   More needs she the divine than the physician.
   God, God forgive us all! Look after her;
   Remove from her the means of all annoyance,
   And still keep eyes upon her. So, good-night:
   My mind she has mated, and amazed my sight.                  75
   I think, but dare not speak.

LADY-IN-WAITING:           Good-night, good doctor. [*Exeunt.*

## SCENE TWO

*Enter, with drum and colours,* MENTEITH, CAITHNESS,
   ANGUS, LENNOX *and* Soldiers.

MENTEITH: The English power is near, led on by Malcolm,
   His uncle Siward, and the good Macduff.
   Revenges burn in them; for their dear causes
   Would to the bleeding and the grim alarm

5 *Excite the . . . man* arouse even a dead man.

6 *well* probably.

8–11 Lennox, despite his mistrust of Macbeth at 3.6, stood guard outside the witches' cavern at 4.1: he is now an active and responsible rebel.

8 *file* list.

10 *unrough* smooth-chinned, too young to shave.

11 *Protest their . . . manhood* proclaim for the first time that they are grown men.

15–16 *buckle . . . rule* restrain his frenzied illness from breaking out of his self-control; also, keep his corrupted kingdom under discipline.

17 *sticking,* like gore. Which episodes in the play does this recall?

18 *now every minute desertions* accuse him of his own breach of faith (when he committed treason against Duncan).

19 *in command* under order.

21–2 See 1.3.108–9. Did Macbeth's 'strange garments' ever 'cleave . . . to their mould' (1.3.145)?

23 his frayed nerves from recoiling and jumping (in fits of madness or 'valiant fury' as at 13–14).

24–5 *When all . . . there* when all aspects of his nature are in revolt against him. Menteith links Macbeth's frenzy with pangs of conscience.

27 *the medicine* the physician, Malcolm. *sickly weal* sick commonwealth.

28 *in our country's purge* to purify our country. They would sacrifice every drop of their blood to expel the fever from Scotland. (Bleeding used to be a treatment for fever.)

30 *dew* water. *sovereign* royal; also, supreme among herbal medicines. Malcolm, the flower of kingship, will cure his country's disease. Note Shakespeare's introduction of the inevitable progress of good.

Excite the mortified man.

ANGUS:                            Near Birnam wood          5
  Shall we well meet them; that way are they coming.

CAITHNESS: Who knows if Donalbain be with his brother?

LENNOX: For certain, sir, he is not: I have a file
  Of all the gentry: there is Siward's son,
  And many unrough youths that even now          10
  Protest their first of manhood.

MENTEITH:                     What does the tyrant?

CAITHNESS: Great Dunsinane he strongly fortifies.
  Some say he's mad; others, that lesser hate him,
  Do call it valiant fury; but for certain
  He cannot buckle his distempered cause          15
  Within the belt of rule.

ANGUS:                  Now does he feel
  His secret murders sticking on his hands;
  Now minutely revolts upbraid his faith-breach;
  Those he commands move only in command,
  Nothing in love: now does he feel his title          20
  Hang loose about him, like a giant's robe
  Upon a dwarfish thief.

MENTEITH:                  Who then shall blame
  His pestered senses to recoil and start,
  When all that is within him does condemn
  Itself for being there?

CAITHNESS:              Well, march we on,          25
  To give obedience where 'tis truly owed:
  Meet we the medicine of the sickly weal,
  And with him pour we, in our country's purge,
  Each drop of us.

LENNOX:          Or so much as it needs
  To dew the sovereign flower and drown the weeds.          30
  Make we our march towards Birnam. [*Exeunt, marching.*

## In Macbeth's castle at Dunsinane

Caithness, Angus and Menteith have described the frenzy of
Macbeth: now it appears in his violent scorn and overweening
confidence, which alternate with profound depression. He looks
more distraught than he did in 4.1.

1 *let them fly all* let all my thanes desert me.
3 *taint with* be weakened by.
4 *the spirits* who spoke through the apparitions in 4.1. Macbeth
bases all his hopes on their slippery words.
5 *consequence* future event.
8 *epicures* self-indulgent weaklings.
9 *sway* control myself.

10 *sag* droop.
11 *loon* rogue. Why is Macbeth so furious? Is he full of foreboding at the servant's pallor, and consequently afraid himself? Is
he 'mad', aroused by 'valiant fury', or terribly worried about
Lady Macbeth?
11–13 The servant, embodiment of fear (who comes as if to test
Macbeth's boast at 9–10), has a face like goose-flesh. He is so
terrified that he can hardly speak, and perhaps his stuttering
effort to begin *Soldier* sounds like the hiss of geese.

15 *lily-livered* cowardly. The liver was thought to be the seat of
courage. *patch* clown.

17 *counsellors* advisers. *to fear* to other people to be afraid.
*whey* skim-milk.
19 Seton is Macbeth's armour-bearer. Macbeth suddenly shouts
for him, then lapses into gloom.
20 *push* crisis.
21 *cheer* hearten; also, chair—enthrone—which was probably
pronounced very like 'cheer' in Shakespeare's day, when the
pun would therefore have been obvious. *disseat* dethrone.
20–1 *This push . . . now.* Does Macbeth speak this sentence with
dread, eagerness, resignation, fortitude, panic?
23 *sere* dry, withered state.
25 *As* such as.
27 *mouth-honour* lip-service.

## SCENE THREE

*Enter* MACBETH, Doctor, *and* Attendants.

MACBETH: Bring me no more reports; let them fly all:
  Till Birnam wood remove to Dunsinane
  I cannot taint with fear. What's the boy Malcolm?
  Was he not born of woman? The spirits that know
  All mortal consequence have pronounced me thus:     *5*
  'Fear not, Macbeth; no man that's born of woman
  Shall e'er have power upon thee.' Then fly, false Thanes,
  And mingle with the English epicures:
  The mind I sway by and the heart I bear
  Shall never sag with doubt nor shake with fear.     *10*

*Enter a* Servant.

  The devil damn thee black, thou cream-faced loon!
  Where got'st thou that goose look?
SERVANT: There is ten thousand . . .
MACBETH:                   Geese, villain?
SERVANT:                           Soldiers, sir.
MACBETH: Go, prick thy face and over-red thy fear,
  Thou lily-livered boy. What soldiers, patch?     *15*
  Death of thy soul! those linen cheeks of thine
  Are counsellors to fear. What soldiers, whey-face?
SERVANT: The English force, so please you.
MACBETH: Take thy face hence. [*Exit* Servant.] Seton!—I
    am sick at heart,
  When I behold—Seton, I say!—This push     *20*
  Will cheer me ever, or disseat me now.
  I have lived long enough: my way of life
  Is fall'n into the sere, the yellow leaf;
  And that which should accompany old age,
  As honour, love, obedience, troops of friends,     *25*
  I must not look to have; but, in their stead,
  Curses, not loud but deep, mouth-honour, breath,

**28** *fain deny* gladly withhold

**19-28** Macbeth regrets that his life is empty and friendless, but he shows no remorse for what he has done. Do you pity him?

**35** *skirr* scour.

**36** *Give me mine armour.* Macbeth repeats this command violently. Seton fetches the armour, and begins putting it on Macbeth at line 48.

**37** Why does Macbeth only now address the doctor?

**38** *thick-coming* teeming.

**42** rub out the troubles written on the mind.

**43** *oblivious* causing forgetfulness.

**44** *stuffed* overburdened.

**46** *himself.* Does the doctor suspect that Macbeth has been asking about his own psychological needs as well as Lady Macbeth's? The doctor's words provoke Macbeth to violence of speech and gesture.

**47-50** Macbeth addresses the doctor and Seton alternately.

**47** *physic* medicine. *I'll none of it* I'll have nothing to do with it.

**48** *staff* commander's baton.

**50** *sir* Seton (who is busy arming him). *dispatch* hurry.

**50-1** *cast the water* diagnose the disease by inspection of urine.

**51** Macbeth emphasizes 'land' and 'her': if only the doctor could cure Scotland! Macbeth has already dismissed Lady Macbeth from his mind.

**52** *pristine* former. When was Scotland last sound in health?

**54** *Pull't off.* Macbeth capriciously orders Seton to pull off the armour.

**55** Some oriental types of rhubarb, and the leaves of senna, are laxatives: they purge the system, and are therefore 'purgative' drugs.

**50-6** A medical metaphor for the campaign was used at 5.2.26-30. What is the difference between Macbeth's tone and that of Caithness and Lennox?

**56** *Hear'st thou of them?* In this sarcastic question he sneers at the doctor for being powerless to help.

**58** *something.* The doctor is sarcastic in reply.

Which the poor heart would fain deny, and dare not.
Seton!

*Enter* SETON.

SETON: What's your gracious pleasure?

MACBETH:                              What news more?   *30*

SETON: All is confirmed, my lord, which was reported.

MACBETH: I'll fight till from my bones my flesh be hacked.
   Give me my armour.

SETON:                          'Tis not needed yet.

MACBETH: I'll put it on.
   Send out more horses, skirr the country round;   *35*
   Hang those that talk of fear. Give me mine armour.
   How does your patient, doctor?

DOCTOR:                            Not so sick, my lord,
   As she is troubled with thick-coming fancies
   That keep her from her rest.

MACBETH:                        Cure her of that:
   Canst thou not minister to a mind diseased,   *40*
   Pluck from the memory a rooted sorrow,
   Raze out the written troubles of the brain,
   And with some sweet oblivious antidote
   Cleanse the stuffed bosom of that perilous stuff
   Which weighs upon the heart?

DOCTOR:                          Therein the patient   *45*
   Must minister to himself.

MACBETH: Throw physic to the dogs—I'll none of it.
   Come, put mine armour on; give me my staff.
   Seton, send out—Doctor, the thanes fly from me.—
   Come, sir, dispatch.—If thou couldst, doctor, cast   *50*
   The water of my land, find her disease,
   And purge it to a sound and pristine health,
   I would applaud thee to the very echo,
   That should applaud again.—Pull't off, I say.—
   What rhubarb, senna, or what purgative drug   *55*
   Would scour these English hence? Hear'st thou of them?

DOCTOR: Ay, my good lord: your royal preparation
   Makes us hear something.

58 *it*. Macbeth's unpredictable state is shown clearly in his orders about his armour.

59 *bane* destruction.

61 *clear* untainted by evil, as well as in safety.
Examine the reasons for the poetic power of 22–8 and 40–5.


### The country near Birnam

The English and rebel Scottish forces have united and now march together. Their controlled power can be shown by formal grouping.

2 *That chambers . . . safe* when people can live safely in their homes (without fear of being murdered in their beds, as Duncan was). *nothing* not at all.

7 *discovery* Macbeth's scouts.
5–8 See the third apparition and his prophecy at 4.1.86–94.

9 *no other but* no other news than that.
10 *endure our . . . before't* allow us to besiege it.

12 *advantage* opportunity.

13 *more and less* high and low. *given him the revolt* deserted him.

14 *constrained things* conscripted wretches. Malcolm speaks scornfully.

15–16 *Let our . . . event* let our opinions, so that they can be justified, wait until the actual outcome. Macduff checks Malcolm's boyish optimism.

16–17 *put we . . . soldiership* let us take full military precautions.

19 *have* possess in strength. *owe* lack in strength.

MACBETH: Bring it after me.
 I will not be afraid of death and bane
 Till Birnam forest come to Dunsinane.     *60*
       [*Exeunt all but the* Doctor.
DOCTOR: Were I from Dunsinane away and clear,
 Profit again should hardly draw me here.   [*Exit.*


## SCENE FOUR

*Enter, with drum and colours,* MALCOLM, *Old* SIWARD *and
his* Son, MACDUFF, MENTEITH, CAITHNESS, ANGUS, LENNOX,
ROSS *and* Soldiers, *marching.*

MALCOLM: Cousins, I hope the days are near at hand
 That chambers will be safe.
MENTEITH:      We doubt it nothing.
OLD SIWARD: What wood is this before us?
MENTEITH: The wood of Birnam.
MALCOLM: <u>Let every soldier hew him down a bough</u>  *5*
 <u>And bear't before him: thereby shall we shadow</u>
 <u>The numbers of our host, and make discovery</u>
 <u>Err in report of us.</u>
SOLDIERS:       It shall be done.
OLD SIWARD: We learn no other but the confident tyrant
 Keeps still in Dunsinane, and will endure   *10*
 Our setting down before't.
MALCOLM:     'Tis his main hope;
 For where there is advantage to be gone,
 Both more and less have given him the revolt,
 And none serve with him but constrained things
 Whose hearts are absent too.
MACDUFF:     Let our just censures  *15*
 Attend the true event, and put we on
 Industrious soldiership.
OLD SIWARD:     The time approaches
 That will with due decision make us know
 What we shall say we have and what we owe.

20 surmises tell of uncertain hopes.
21 but strokes must settle the real issue.
15-22 Why are Macduff and Siward more cautious than Malcolm?
Drumming accompanies the exit.


*Macbeth's castle at Dunsinane*

This entry is ragged and wild, in contrast to the disciplined movement which ended the previous scene.


3 *them* the besiegers.
4 *ague* (two syllables) fever.
5 *forced* reinforced.
6 *dareful* boldly. *beard to beard* face to face in battle.


8 Seton speaks with fear.

10-11 *The time . . . night-shriek* there was a time when I would
have gone cold when I heard a cry in the night. How did he
react to the nocturnal cries in 2.2?
11 *fell of hair* scalp with the hair on it.
12 *dismal treatise* sinister story.
13 *As life were in't* as if it were alive.
14 *Direness* horror.
15 *Cannot once . . . me* can never startle me now.
9-15 *I have . . . me.* Does he speak of his change with regret,
satisfaction, astonishment, repentance, blank unconcern?
16 Why do we suspect suicide?
17 He is too apathetic even to ask how she died, and he does not
pray for her. Compare 4.3.226.
18 *a time . . . word* a time convenient for such news.
19 What is the effect of this line?

Thoughts speculative their unsure hopes relate,    20
But certain issue strokes must arbitrate:
<u>Towards which advance the war.</u>

                   *[Exeunt, marching.*


## SCENE FIVE

*Enter, with a drum and colours, MACBETH, SETON,*
*and Soldiers.*

MACBETH: Hang out our banners on the outward walls;
  The cry is still 'They come!' Our castle's strength
  Will laugh a siege to scorn: here let them lie
  Till famine and the ague eat them up;
  Were they not forced with those that should be ours,    5
  We might have met them dareful, beard to beard,
  And beat them backward home.

                 *[A cry of women within.*
              What is that noise?
SETON: It is the cry of women, my good lord.     *[Exit.*
MACBETH: I have almost forgot the taste of fears.
  The time has been my senses would have cooled    10
  To hear a night-shriek, and my fell of hair
  Would at a dismal treatise rouse and stir
  As life were in't. I have supped full with horrors;
  Direness, familiar to my slaughterous thoughts,
  Cannot once start me.

              *Re-enter SETON.*

             Wherefore was that cry?    15
SETON: The Queen, my lord, is dead.
MACBETH: She should have died hereafter;
  There would have been a time for such a word.
  Tomorrow, and tomorrow, and tomorrow,
  Creeps in this petty pace from day to day,    20

               [ 159 ]  *with her death goes all*
                        *meaning of life*

*No meaning of life* (margin note beside line 17)

**21** until the book of life ends and time vanishes in eternity.

**22-3** *all our yesterdays . . . death* every day of our lives has served as some poor fool's candle, lighting him to bed in his grave. Compare Job 8: 9: 'For we are but of yesterday, and are ignorant: for our days upon earth are but a shadow.' *lighted, candle.* Job. 18: 6 says of the fate of the wicked: 'The light shall be dark in his dwelling, and his candle shall be put out with him.'

**24** *poor,* to be pitied because of the shortness of his part.

**25** *frets his* distresses himself during his.

**18-28** From *word* the imagery extends in *syllable, heard, tale* and *sound,* and from *creeps* in *pace, way, walking* and *struts.* These two strands of imagery are intervowen with others of time and light. All end in *nothing.* Macbeth finds life meaningless and contemptible because by now his sins have bled all meaning and glory out of it.

**28** There is a long pause before Macbeth addresses the tongue-tied messenger.

**35** Macbeth is aroused into a frenzy of fear, but the messenger stubbornly persists. Does Macbeth strike him?

**40** *famine cling thee* you shrivel with starvation. *sooth* truth.

**42** *pall* fail. He is thinking aloud, not addressing anyone.

**43-4** *equivocation of . . . truth.* In his dawning disillusion, Macbeth echoes the porter's lines 2.3.8-11.

**46** *Arm . . . out!* He gives Seton orders for a sortie from the castle, then lapses into meditation again.

**47** *avouches* asserts.

**49** *'gin* begin.

**50** *estate* order. If he is going to be killed, then he wants the world to be destroyed with him; see his destructive defiance at 3.2.16 and 4.1.58-60.

**51** *wrack* wreck (as at 1.3.114).

**52** *harness* armour.

**51-2** Macbeth rouses himself: the couplet, harsh in sound, sums up his desperate valour. It can be acted to recall the early Macbeth, called up by the appropriate circumstance—battle. This can give an upsurge of pity, as we realize the extent of Macbeth's degradation, and heighten the effect of the catastrophe.

The bell begins to ring for the sortie as his soldiers hurry after him: in the Globe Theatre, the same bell would have rung at at 2.3.80, and its sound now might be a significant reminder of Duncan's death.

To the last syllable of recorded time;
And all our yesterdays have lighted fools
The way to dusty death. Out, out, brief candle!
Life's but a walking shadow, a poor player
That struts and frets his hour upon the stage,          *25*
And then is heard no more: it is a tale
Told by an idiot, full of sound and fury
Signifying nothing.

*Enter a* Messenger.

Thou com'st to use thy tongue; thy story quickly.
MESSENGER: Gracious my lord,                              *30*
  I should report that which I say I saw,
  But know not how to do it.
MACBETH:                        Well, say, sir.
MESSENGER: As I did stand my watch upon the hill,
  I looked toward Birnam, and anon methought
  The wood began to move.
MACBETH:                        Liar and slave!          *35*
MESSENGER: Let me endure your wrath, if't be not so:
  Within this three mile may you see it coming;
  I say, a moving grove.
MACBETH:                     If thou speak'st false,
Upon the next tree shalt thou hang alive,
Till famine cling thee: if thy speech be sooth,          *40*
I care not if thou dost for me as much.
I pall in resolution, and begin
To doubt the equivocation of the fiend          Banquo says this
That lies like truth: 'Fear not, till Birnam wood    Act 1 scene 3 line 123
Do come to Dunsinane.' And now a wood                     *45*
Comes toward Dunsinane. Arm, arm, and out!
If this which he avouches does appear,
There is nor flying hence nor tarrying here.
I 'gin to be aweary of the sun,
And wish the estate o'the world were now undone.          *50*
Ring the alarum-bell! Blow, wind! come, wrack!
At least we'll die with harness on our back.
                              [*Exeunt. Alarums.*

As shown in the drawing opposite, nondescript costumes—
which could be used again from play to play—sufficed for non-
speaking actors on Shakespeare's stage. An important character,
such as Malcolm, wore armour in the military scenes. The episode
with the boughs was staged in a simple, conventional way.

### Outside the castle

Orderly drumbeats and Malcolm's calm speech contrast with
Macbeth's overwhelming despair.

1 *leavy* leafy.
2 The soldiers discard their camouflage, and reveal themselves.
    *uncle* Old Siward.
4 *battle* division of the army. *we* the royal plural.
5 *upon's* upon us.
6 *order* plan.

7 *Do we but* if we only. *power* troops.

10 *harbingers* forerunners; see 1.4.45. The trumpets sound as
    the scene ends.

## SCENE SIX

*Enter, with drum and colours,* MALCOLM, *Old* SIWARD,
MACDUFF *and their Army, with boughs.*

MALCOLM: Now near enough; your leavy screens throw down,
    And show like those you are. You, worthy uncle,
    Shall with my cousin, your right-noble son,
    Lead our first battle: worthy Macduff and we
    Shall take upon's what else remains to do,     5
    According to our order.
OLD SIWARD:               Fare you well.
    Do we but find the tyrant's power tonight,
    Let us be beaten, if we cannot fight.
MACDUFF: Make all our trumpets speak; give them all
    breath,
    Those clamorous harbingers of blood and death.     10
                         *[Exeunt.*

### *Another part of the field outside the castle*

Drums and trumpets sound a call to arms.

1 *tied . . . stake,* like a bear to be baited by mastiffs.

2 *course* bout. *What's he* what sort of a man is he.

11 *S.D.* This is a short fight. Does Macbeth's killing of young Siward seem praiseworthy or despicable?

12–13 Macbeth's victory has increased the rashness of his confidence.

13 *S.D.* Alarums. The sequence of battle-scenes is like a sequence of cinema-shots, mostly very brief. Fighting on a large scale, which could be filmed in long-shots, cannot be shown in the theatre, but it can be made audible by 'alarums'—tumult of trumpets, drums, shouts and the clash of swords off-stage. They therefore punctuate the action of these scenes.

Young Siward's body can now be removed by soldiers, or it can remain, unseen by old Siward, whose contented speech, 24–8, then gains poignancy.

16 *still* for ever.

17 *kerns.* Like Macdonwald at 1.2.13, Macbeth has to rely on Irish mercenaries.

18 *staves* spear-shafts. *either thou, Macbeth* either I strike at you, Macbeth.

20 *undeeded* unused. *shouldst be* art likely to be.

## SCENE SEVEN

*Alarums. Enter* MACBETH. *become an animal.*

MACBETH: They have tied me to a stake; I cannot fly,
But bear-like I must fight the course. What's he
That was not born of woman? Such a one *He admits to*
Am I to fear, or none. *doubts of witches but still holds on to the last prophecies.*

*Enter Young* SIWARD.

YOUNG SIWARD: What is thy name?

MACBETH:                        Thou'lt be afraid to hear it.    5

YOUNG SIWARD: No; though thou call'st thyself a hotter
name
Than any is in hell.

MACBETH:            My name's Macbeth.

YOUNG SIWARD: The devil himself could not pronounce a
title
More hateful to mine ear.

MACBETH:                No, nor more fearful.

YOUNG SIWARD: Thou liest, abhorred tyrant; with my sword    10
I'll prove the lie thou speak'st.

*[They fight and Young* SIWARD *is slain.*

MACBETH:                Thou wast born of woman.
But swords I smile at, weapons laugh to scorn,
Brandished by man that's of a woman born.            [*Exit.*

*Alarums. Enter* MACDUFF.

MACDUFF: That way the noise is. Tyrant, show thy face!
If thou beest slain and with no stroke of mine,
My wife and children's ghosts will haunt me still.  *Desperate*[15] *to kill Macb.*
I cannot strike at wretched kerns, whose arms *to stop his*
Are hired to bear their staves: either thou, Macbeth, *families ghosts.*
Or else my sword with an unbattered edge
I sheathe again undeeded.

[*Alarums.*
There thou shouldst be;            20

*Macbeth* is difficult to film. The drawing on page 164 shows Maurice Evans in the 1960 version. Many things, besides dangerously heavy swords, can give trouble in stage productions of this great but grim play. It is generally disliked by actors: they believe that to quote from it or even to mention it brings bad luck. But it also brings large audiences.

21 *By*  judging by.
22 *bruited*  proclaimed.
23 *S.D.* Macduff hurries off, sword in hand. The entry of Siward and Malcolm is serenely triumphant.
24 *gently rendered*  surrendered with little resistance.
29 *strike beside*  fight on our side; or, aim to miss.

### Another part of the field

1 *the Roman fool*  the part of a defeated warrior who, like Brutus, Cassius and Mark Antony, killed himself in the Roman tradition rather than fall into enemy hands.
2 *lives*  live enemies.

4 *Of all men else*  more than all others. Macbeth remembers 4.1.71–2.
5 *charged*  burdened (as at 5.1.50).
5–6 *But get . . . already.*  Does regret or foreboding prompt Macbeth to say this? His lack of frank and full repentance contrasts with Cawdor's final confession as reported by Malcolm, 1.4.3–11.
8 *terms*  words. The fighters draw apart for a breather, and then Macbeth speaks.
9 *mayst*  canst. *intrenchant*  uncuttable.
10 *impress*  make an impression on.
12 *must not*  cannot.

By this great clatter, one of greatest note
Seems bruited. Let me find him, Fortune!
And more I beg not.                    [*Exit. Alarums.*

*Enter* MALCOLM *and Old* SIWARD.

OLD SIWARD: This way, my lord; the castle's gently rendered:
  The tyrant's people on both sides do fight,                    25
  The noble thanes do bravely in the war,
  The day almost itself professes yours,
  And little is to do.
MALCOLM:                    We have met with foes
  That strike beside us.
OLD SIWARD: Enter, sir, the castle.            [*Exeunt. Alarums.*


## SCENE EIGHT

*Enter* MACBETH.

MACBETH: Why should I play the Roman fool, and die
  On mine own sword? whiles I see lives, the gashes
  Do better upon them.

*Enter* MACDUFF.

MACDUFF:            Turn, hell-hound, turn!
MACBETH: Of all men else I have avoided thee:
  But get thee back, my soul is too much charged              5
  With blood of thine already.
MACDUFF:                    I have no words—
  My voice is in my sword, thou bloodier villain
  Than terms can give thee out!            [*They fight.*
MACBETH:                    Thou losest labour.
  As easy mayst thou the intrenchant air
  With thy keen sword impress as make me bleed:              10
  Let fall thy blade on vulnerable crests,
  I bear a charmed life, which must not yield
  To one of woman born.

13 *Despair* despair of. *charm* the charm on your life.
14 *angel* evil angel. *still* ever.

16 *Untimely* prematurely. See the second apparition and his prophecy at 4.1.77–81.
18 *better part of man* manly spirit.
19 *juggling* cheating.
20 *palter* equivocate.
22 *it . . . hope* the meaning which our hope had found in the promise. *I'll not . . . thee.* Macbeth is overcome with fear, despite his lack of feeling at 5.5.9.
24 *gaze o' the time* popular spectacle.

25 *monsters* freaks shown at fairs.
26 *advertised* by a painting hung from a pole, with this caption.
27 *Here,* in the booth behind the advertisement.
27–9 Is Macbeth's proud refusal to yield consistent with his character elsewhere in the play?
29 *baited,* as a bear would be.
31 *opposed* set as my opponent.
32 *try the last* fight to the end.
33 *Lay on* fight on.
34 *'Hold, enough!'* This is like the cry of heralds stopping a tourney.
S.D. Shakespeare's contemporaries, being swordsmen, demanded good stage-fights. This contest makes a thrilling climax to the play, with the fighters leaving the stage in full combat, continuing their battle audibly behind the scenes, and returning on another part of the stage for the final blows. Macbeth's body is removed by soldiers.

*Inside the castle*

The trumpets sound a retreat and then play a victorious flourish.

2 *go off* be killed, a euphemism like Macbeth's at 1.7.20 and 3.1.105, from an actor leaving the stage. *by . . . see* to judge by these I see around me.

[ 168 ]

MACDUFF:                    Despair thy charm;
  And let the angel whom thou still hast served
  Tell thee, Macduff was from his mother's womb          15
  Untimely ripped.
MACBETH: Accursed be that tongue that tells me so,
  For it hath cowed my better part of man!
  And be these juggling fiends no more believed,
  That palter with us in a double sense,                 20
  That keep the word of promise to our ear,
  And break it to our hope. I'll not fight with thee.
MACDUFF: Then yield thee, coward,
  And live to be the show and gaze o'the time.
  We'll have thee, as our rarer monsters are,            25
  Painted upon a pole, and underwrit,
  'Here may you see the tyrant.'
MACBETH:                    I will not yield,
  To kiss the ground before young Malcolm's feet,
  And to be baited with the rabble's curse.
  Though Birnam wood be come to Dunsinane,               30
  And thou opposed, being of no woman born,
  Yet I will try the last. Before my body
  I throw my war-like shield. Lay on, Macduff,
  And damned be him that first cries 'Hold, enough!'
                              [*Exeunt, fighting. Alarums.*
          *Re-enter fighting, and* MACBETH *is slain.*
                                        [*Exit* MACDUFF.


SCENE NINE

*Retreat and flourish. Enter, with drum and colours,*
  MALCOLM, *Old* SIWARD, ROSS, Lords *and* Soldiers.

MALCOLM: I would the friends we miss were safe arrived.
OLD SIWARD: Some must go off; and yet, by these I see,
  So great a day as this is cheaply bought.
MALCOLM: Macduff is missing, and your noble son.
ROSS: Your son, my lord, has paid a soldier's debt:      5

8 in the post where he fought without flinching.

12 *Had he . . . before?* Old Siward, the warrior, wants to know that his son died valiantly.

14 *hairs,* a pun on 'heirs'. It expresses stoic pride, and may be a reminder of Macbeth's lack of an heir.

16 *knolled* tolled.

18 *parted well* died manfully. *paid his score* honourably paid his debts, by doing his duty.

13–19 Old Siward's approval of his son's death implies that honourable self-sacrifice is a fine thing. Macbeth might have remained a loyal officer, faithfully serving Duncan.

19 *S.D.* See the first apparition and his warning at 4.1.68–72.

21 *the time is free* the age is set free.

22 *compassed with . . . pearl* surrounded by the jewels of your country. The nobles are like pearls encircling a crown.

27 *reckon with your several loves* reward the love of each one of you.

28 *make us . . . you* cancel our debt to you. He does this in the next line.

30 *In such . . . named* named with this honourable title. Malcolm creates the first Scottish earls. *What's . . . do* what more is to be done.

31 which wants to be started afresh with the new era.

He only lived but till he was a man,
The which no sooner had his prowess confirmed
In the unshrinking station where he fought,
But like a man he died.

OLD SIWARD:                    Then he is dead?

ROSS: Ay, and brought off the field. Your cause of sorrow      10
    Must not be measured by his worth, for then
    It hath no end.

OLD SIWARD:          Had he his hurts before?

ROSS: Ay, on the front.

OLD SIWARD:               Why then, God's soldier be he!
    Had I as many sons as I have hairs,
    I would not wish them to a fairer death:                    15
    And so his knell is knolled.

MALCOLM:                       He's worth more sorrow,
    And that I'll spend for him.

OLD SIWARD:                     He's worth no more.
    They say he parted well and paid his score:
    And so God be with him! Here comes newer comfort.

*Enter* MACDUFF, *with* MACBETH'S *head on a spear.*

MACDUFF: Hail, King! for so thou art. Behold, where stands     20
    The usurper's cursed head: the time is free:
    I see thee compassed with thy kingdom's pearl,
    That speak my salutation in their minds;
    Whose voices I desire aloud with mine—
    Hail, King of Scotland!

ALL:                       Hail, King of Scotland!            25
                                          [*Flourish.*

MALCOLM: We shall not spend a large expense of time
    Before we reckon with your several loves,
    And make us even with you. My Thanes and kinsmen,
    Henceforth be Earls, the first that ever Scotland
    In such an honour named. What's more to do,                 30
    Which would be planted newly with the time—
    As calling home our exiled friends abroad
    That fled the snares of watchful tyranny;

34 *Producing forth*  bringing out of hiding.

35 To what extent does Malcolm's estimate of Macbeth and Lady Macbeth coincide with yours?

36 *by self and*  by her own. The doctor's fears, at 5.1.72-4, have been fulfilled.

38 *Grace*  God.

39 *in measure*  in due proportion.

Note the quiet tone that concludes the play, comparable to the peaceful chord at the end of many tumultuous pieces of music. Life must go on and the humdrum tenor of the everyday world be renewed.

Producing forth the cruel ministers
Of this dead butcher and his fiend-like queen,    35
Who, as 'tis thought, by self and violent hands
Took off her life—this, and what needful else
That calls upon us, by the grace of Grace
We will perform in measure, time, and place:
So, thanks to all at once and to each one,    40
Whom we invite to see us crown'd at Scone.
                    [*Flourish. Exeunt.*

# INDEX TO NOTES

# *Index*